THE LIFE-GIVING SWORD

THE LIFE-GIVING SWORD

*Secret Teachings from
the House of the Shogun*

Yagyu Munenori

<small>TRANSLATED BY</small> William Scott Wilson

Shambhala
Boulder
2012

THIS TRANSLATION IS DEDICATED TO
JOHN PINKERTON SISCOE

Note: Throughout this volume, Japanese names appear in the traditional
order, surname preceding given name.

Frontispiece: Samurai (Bushi), from the series Ten Kinds of People
(detail). Photograph © 2012 Museum of Fine Arts, Boston.

Shambhala Publications, Inc.
2129 13th Street
Boulder, Colorado 80302
www.shambhala.com

9 8 7 6 5 4

Printed in the United States of America

♾ This edition is printed on acid-free paper that meets
the American National Standards Institute Z39.48 Standard.
♻ This book is printed on 30% postconsumer recycled paper.
For more information please visit www.shambhala.com.

Shambhala Publications is distributed worldwide
by Penguin Random House, Inc., and its subsidiaries.

Library of Congress Cataloging-in-Publication Data

Yagyu, Munenori, 1571–1646.
[Hyoho kadensho. English]
The life-giving sword: secret teachings from the house of the Shogun.
Yagyu Munenori / translated by William Scott Wilson.
p. cm.
Includes bibliographical references.
ISBN 978-1-59030-990-2 (pbk.)
1. Swordplay—Japan—Philosophy—Early works to 1800. 2. Military art
and science—Japan—Early works to 1800. I. Wilson, William Scott,
1944– II. Title.
U101.Y3413 2012
796.86—dc23
2012017267

CONTENTS

PREFACE

In the storehouse of a temple called the Hotokuji, there is a wooden statue of a man in his sixties or seventies seated in the classic posture of knees out and feet drawn together. The lacquer coloring of his robes has chipped here and there indicating the age of the statue, but the overall impression is one of a character both robust and intense. The man's neck is remarkably thick, indicating excellent health, and his eyes show intelligence and deep introspection. His lips, under a thin moustache, are full, and seem ready to give expression to his thoughts. The hilt of a sword appears almost as an afterthought at his left. All in all, this is a man to be reckoned with, inspiring not exactly fear, but great respect from his implicit authority and knowledge.

Somewhere there is a hard edge to his personality; and somewhere, in no particular place, a sense of suppressed wistfulness.

In the early years of the Edo period (1603–1868), a time of intense development of the martial arts, there appeared three short treatises on swordsmanship that would be influential far beyond the promise of their few pages.

The first was *The Mysterious Record of Unmoving Wisdom* (*Fudochi shinmyoroku*), written by Zen priest Takuan Soho in about 1632. This was primarily a philosophical piece looking at swordsmanship from the perspective of Zen Buddhism, especially emphasizing the desirability of keeping the mind free from attachment and fixation. In terms of combat, this meant keeping the mind from stopping, or "abiding" anywhere—whether the stance, technique, the opponent's sword, or anything that would keep your mind from moving freely. To stop the mind, Takuan declared, would mean defeat.

Although he came from a samurai family himself, Takuan may have been aided in his understanding of the martial arts by swordsman-artist Miyamoto Musashi. In 1629, Takuan had been exiled to the far northern province of Dewa for his public disagreement with a Tokugawa government policy on the rights of ecclesiastical succession. In Dewa he was put under the charge of the local daimyo, Lord Matsudaira. In 1631, Musashi visited the same area to exhibit his style with the sword at the invitation of a certain Matsudaira Dewa no kami. If this was indeed the same daimyo, there can be little doubt that the lord would have introduced the two talented men and enjoyed a night or perhaps a few days of discussion and perhaps even a demonstration of the application of Zen to swordsmanship. Strong similarities in the fundamental assumptions held by Takuan and Musashi vis-à-vis the art of combat would seem to confirm this meeting, if not in Dewa, then perhaps elsewhere.

The second influential book (the third chronologically) was Musashi's own work, *The Book of Five Rings* (*Gorin no sho*), written between 1643 and 1645. Unlike Takuan's philosophical treatise, Musashi's book took a practical approach to swordsmanship, informing the reader of such tactics as how to move the feet, where to stand in terms of the sun or other light sources, and how to parry and thrust. The point of entering into confrontation, according to Musashi, was not to die with one's weapon at one's side or employed in a flashy but ineffective technique, but to win. The underlying frame of mind of the art, however, was just as important to Musashi as to Takuan, and this was to set the mind free, never allowing it to stop, even after the opponent seemed to be defeated.

This undeterred, continually moving mind is artistically and philosophically symbolized by the Buddhist avatar Fudo Myo-o (Unmoving Brightness King), often depicted holding in one hand a sword that he uses to cut through our ignorance and in the other a rope to tie up our passions; with these he sets our True Mind free. It is perhaps not a coincidence that Takuan dedicated a part of his work to the description of Fudo, while Musashi, an accomplished artist, sculpted an astonishing statue of this Buddhist inspiration that still fills the observer with awe.

The final classical work on swordsmanship—offered in translation in this volume—was *Heiho kadensho* (*The Life-Giving Sword*;

sometimes referred to as *The Book of Clan Traditions on the Martial Arts*) written by Yagyu Munenori in 1632 or soon thereafter. While Takuan's work emphasizes the Zen approach to swordsmanship and Musashi's the practical, Munenori attempted to walk a fine line between the two extremes, and to present both a philosophical groundwork for practice and some of the actual practices themselves.

The philosophy or psychology of the work is based for the most part on *The Mysterious Record of Unmoving Wisdom*, which was written for Munenori by his friend and mentor Takuan. Munenori places a similar emphasis on keeping the mind free of attachments, or in his terms, the "sicknesses" accrued by too much attention to technique or even to the idea of winning. His cure for such sicknesses was, paradoxically, even more of the same, used much as a wedge might be used to dislodge another wedge stuck in place. Intense self-discipline and a deep understanding of the principles of Zen are the keys to becoming an "accomplished" man of the Way.

The practices themselves Munenori inherited from a long line of predecessors, including his father—the artistic and refined Sekishusai—and his father's almost legendary teacher, Kamiizumi Ise no kami Hidetsuna. Each of these men made improvements on the techniques that he had received and passed the techniques down with the challenge to refine them even further. Munenori, it is said, brought these techniques, which included the famous No-Sword, to their perfection and transmitted them to his students as the Yagyu Shinkage-ryu school of the martial arts. It is perhaps indicative of the effectiveness of this school that one of its most enthusiastic students was the third Tokugawa shogun, Iemitsu, a man who wasted little time on pursuits that failed to bring practical results.

Munenori stands in perfect contrast to his contemporary, Miyamoto Musashi, who seemed to come out of nowhere to become famous for his extraordinary victories while adamantly defining himself as having been taught by no one. Munenori, on the other hand, clearly had a long heritage, became famous for accomplishments that involved no personal matches, and just as adamantly defined himself by his predecessors, going so far as to sign his pivotal book first with Kamiizumi's name, then his father's, and only lastly his own.

Heiho kadensho is at once a prompt for techniques already learned, a book of carefully worded instructions for further practices, a meditative source for sweeping away the psychological obstacles encountered by the student, and a philosophical basis for using the sword as an instrument of life rather than death.

A man involved in the political administration of his own local fief and that of the Tokugawa government, Munenori saw in the practice of the sword a Way to forge and temper the student into a total human being. Musashi's objective of swordsmanship was to "win," although that "winning" included an ability to understand and perform in any Way whatsoever. Munenori's approach was from a different angle: on the basis of observation of his father and the teachings of Takuan, he defined his objective as one "sustaining" or "giving life" in a complete sense. The *Heiho kadensho* offers a path of study to that objective through the practice of the sword, the sharp edge of which must learn to express the blossoming of flowers in the spring and the withering of the leaves in fall.

Heiho kadensho is considered the central text of the Yagyu Shinkage-ryu, but is by no means the only work concerned with the tenets of that school. Munenori himself wrote other short works on the subject; his father, Sekishusai, wrote a catalog of techniques and poetry about both his own style and the martial arts in general; and his son, Mitsuyoshi (whom some have viewed as the very best swordsman of the family) wrote several detailed books on his understanding of the Yagyu principles and style. Then there is Zen priest Takuan's *Fudochi shinmyoroku*, which might be considered the *Heiho kadensho*'s philosophical subtext, and another short work of Takuan's, the *Taiaki*. The latter may actually have been written to one of Munenori's contemporaries, Ono no Tadaaki of the Itto-ryu, but Munenori was familiar with either the writing itself or its principles through his discussions with Takuan. I have included notes from these other works with this text as they seemed appropriate to clarify and expand Munenori's thoughts. For both the original text and most of those notes, I have used the *Heiho kadensho* published in 1985 by Iwanami Bunko and edited by Watanabe Ichiro. I am both indebted and grateful to Mr. Watanabe for his own helpful notes and careful scholarship, without which Munenori's work, which is often expressed in difficult Chinese and Buddhist philosophical terms, would be far more difficult to fathom.

I am also grateful to Kuramochi Tetsuo and Elizabeth Floyd, formerly at Kodasha International, for their encouragement and guidance in the original translation project, and to Beth Frankl and John Golebiewski at Shambhala Publications for all the work they have done in this new edition. I owe a special *gassho* to my colleague Dave Lowry, writer and sword practitioner of the Yagyu Shinkage-ryu, for his insightful observations and research suggestions for this project; and to Meik and Diane Skoss for their help and encouragement. To my wife, Emily, I owe a debt of gratitude for her suggestions on the manuscript and for her patience with my virtual disappearance into the translation for several months. Finally and as always, my deep gratitude to my late professors, Hiraga Noburu and Richard McKinnon, concerning whom it is appropriate to paraphrase Iemitsu's words after the passing of Munenori, "If only they were here, I could ask them about this."

Any and all mistakes are my own.

—WILLIAM SCOTT WILSON

INTRODUCTION

In the summer of 1615, the Tokugawa forces had surrounded Osaka Castle and were determined to end the influence of the Toyotomi family and its supporters. The castle was nearly impregnable and was defended by as many as sixty thousand men, although the surrounding troops numbered nearly twice that many. Attacks and counterattacks continued without decisive victories on either side, and despite the overwhelming numbers on the Tokugawa side, the battle seemed stalemated. Time, of course, favored the attackers.

The tedium was broken one day, however, when a desperate force of about twenty to thirty men led by a certain Kimura Shigenari, launched a surprise attack and broke into shogun Tokugawa Hidetada's camp.[1] The shogun's men were thrown into confusion as the assailants, almost incredibly, pressed their way to within a short distance of the shogun himself. There, however, they confronted a middle-aged samurai, who was standing calmly in front of the shogun's horse. The man stepped forward and, with shocking speed, dexterity, and grace, killed seven of the attackers, giving the shogun's guards a chance to regroup and counterattack. Having removed the shogun from danger, he once again took up his post.

The middle-aged samurai was Yagyu Tajima no kami Munenori, sword instructor to the shogun and the man most trusted to be by the shogun's side. Hidetada had been taught patiently many times by Munenori in the dojo, but now his forty-four-year-old teacher had demonstrated swordsmanship to him on the thin line between life and death. One might well imagine the shogun's thoughts later that night, and his resolve to pay a bit more attention to his teacher's instructions during practice. When the castle had fallen and they had returned to Edo, he would grasp his bamboo practice sword with a new sense of purpose.

And what of Munenori?

BEGINNINGS

In 1594, Ieyasu, the future first Tokugawa shogun, was consolidating his plans for what was to come. It would be another four years before the current ruler of Japan, Toyotomi Hideyoshi, would pass away, but the fifty-eight-year-old leader was already showing some signs of mental instability and possibly physical ailments. He was currently obsessed with a risky and costly invasion of Korea and looked forward to the eventual conquest of

Ming China. This adventure, Ieyasu figured, was certain to fail, and when it did, Hideyoshi's position could be fatally weakened.

Ieyasu was a prudent man, not given to taking unnecessary chances. Ideally, he liked to consider all possible outcomes and ramifications of his actions in advance. Alliances with other daimyo were crucial for the large number of forces they could provide in a sudden decisive battle, but Ieyasu also knew that battles were not necessarily won by the side with the greater number of troops. There were times when guerilla warfare was also necessary, and there was always a need for good intelligence gathered by men who could slip in and out of territories unnoticed.

Perhaps most of all, Ieyasu was impressed by loyalty. It was said of his troops that none ever died with his back to the enemy, and this was indicative not only of the care he gave his men but of his skill in choosing his allies from the very start.

Ieyasu was also a talented and enthusiastic swordsman and quite often would begin the day with some practice in the dojo. He was always on the lookout for outstanding teachers.

At some point during the year 1594 Ieyasu felt that he should meet Yagyu Sekishusai Muneyoshi, a man who interested him for a number of reasons. This Sekishusai was considered to be one of the finest swordsmen in the country, and was said to have perfected the technique—attempted by many without success— of defeating an armed man without resorting to the use of any weapon. He had come from landed gentry in a valley in Yamato— not far from the capital, Kyoto—that his family had governed for generations. Interesting to Ieyasu was the fact that Sekishusai had been dispossessed of a large portion of that land in 1585 by the Toyotomi on suspicion of maintaining *kakushiden*, or fields hidden from taxation. Just as important perhaps was that Sekishusai's wife, Shunto Gozen, was a daughter of the Okuhara family, a powerful clan in the nearby area of Iga, famous for the warriors trained in the arts of espionage and assassination called *ninja*.

Sekishusai, then sixty-six years old, was invited one day to visit Ieyasu at his villa of Takagamine, just outside the capital. Sekishusai was accompanied by his twenty-two-year-old son Munenori, who had recently returned from service with the Hosokawa forces in the attack on Odawara Castle. Ieyasu was just fifty-three.

When the two Yagyu men arrived at Takagamine, they were received cordially by Ieyasu, who treated them with great respect. Ieyasu asked with the expertise of an accomplished swordsman about the principles of the Shinkage-ryu as the Yagyu understood them, and inquired specifically and in detail about the No-Sword technique. Impressed by the somewhat mysterious practices explained by both father and son, but unconvinced by a demonstration bout, Ieyasu finally took up a wooden sword himself and requested a match with Sekishusai, who was old but still solid. According to Yagyu tradition, the match went as follows:

> Sekishusai hung both arms so that his elbows were in front of his knees, lowered his body into a ball, and began to

walk about in that manner with no difficulty. Ieyasu straightaway struck at him with a direct blow. As soon as he did, Sekishusai's left fist came up "like a monkey's strong arm" and grabbed the handle of Ieyasu's sword, which the latter was holding with both hands. Instantly, Ieyasu's sword flew into the air, and Sekishusai's left arm enveloped Ieyasu while his right fist lightly thumped his younger adversary's chest. Ieyasu was wearing a camp *haori* over his thick body, and went staggering backwards.

Ieyasu was greatly impressed, but gallantly pressed his guest for a second match. When that contest quickly ended with the same result, Ieyasu apologized for his obstinacy, and admitted defeat. He thereupon presented Sekishusai with a sword forged by the famous smith Kagenori. Perceiving the unique quality of Sekishusai's technique and the maturity of his character, Ieyasu quickly wrote up a teacher/student agreement that included a clause declaring that he would never neglect his relationship with Sekishusai.

When Ieyasu politely asked Sekishusai to serve as his personal instructor, however, the latter demurred on the excuse of his old age, and instead recommended his son Munenori. This agreed upon, Sekishusai returned to Yagyu-mura and became a lay-priest, while Munenori became Ieyasu's sword instructor and personal retainer.

This story is pivotal because it was the karmic seed that would bring Munenori to the position of head of the Yagyu Shinkage-ryu, and because it was one of the two pivotal events in his life that would seal the direction of his career. The other event actually occurred some time before he was born, and for that story it is necessary to turn back a number of years.

In 1559, a swordsman by the name of Kamiizumi Ise no kami Hidetsuna was traveling with his two closest disciples, his son Hidetane and nephew Hikita Kagekane, through the country-side around the old capital of Nara. Kamiizumi was considered one of the most accomplished swordsmen of his day. According to tradition, his instructors included Matsumoto Masanobu (d. 1543?), who was himself said to be a student of the shadowy figure Iizasa Yamashiro no kami Choisai. Matsumoto was from the Kashima tradition of swordsmen and, while participating in over twenty battles, seems never to have taken part in a one-on-one duel. He died from either a spear or arrow wound in battle, possibly at age sixty-seven.

From Matsumoto, Kamiizumi may have learned the *ichi no tachi*, or *hitotsu tachi*, a hair-raising technique of entering the op-ponent's striking range, drawing an attack rather than initiating one, and stepping inside the blow while delivering one's own.[2] This required an extraordinary sense of timing and distance, and did not allow for the smallest miscalculation.

Kamiizumi is also thought to have studied under the legendary Aisu Ikosai (1452–1538), a wandering swordsman who was said to have been involved in piracy along the Korean and Chinese coasts. He based his sword techniques on animal behavior and the rhythm of waves, thus perhaps validating his claim to have studied the art as far away as Ming China. Although the names of styles are often accredited to a number of different personages, Ikosai seems to have been the swordsman who actually developed the Kage-ryu, a style that relied less on mechanical technique than on discerning the movements of the opponent's mind and responding to those movements before they could be translated into actions.

Kamiizumi developed what he had learned from his various instructors into what he called the Shinkage-ryu. A student of Zen, he also developed his "everyday mind" to such a degree and was so even-tempered that his face revealed nothing of what he was thinking or feeling.[3] Even the best swordsmen of the time were unable to judge his skills upon encountering him for the first time.

Kamiizumi was also influenced by the compassion encouraged by Buddhism and by the suffering he had witnessed during the latter part of the Sengoku period. Once, while traveling in Owari Province near the Myokoji Temple, he and his two disciples came upon a crowd of people gathered excitedly near the entrance of a small hut. Upon inquiring into the matter, he was told that a child had been kidnapped by either a thief or an unbalanced man, and for hours had been held inside the hut with a sword to its throat. The villagers could conceive of no plan of rescue, but

Kamiizumi quietly borrowed a priest's robes, had his head shaved, and approached the hut with two riceballs. Understanding that the kidnapper must have been famished after such a long stand-off, he eventually tricked him into reaching for one of the balls of rice. Just at that moment, Kamiizumi leapt into the hut without a weapon of his own, disarmed the man, and freed the child with no harm to anyone.[4]

Kamiizumi had learned from Ikosai and from Matsumoto the importance of placing as much emphasis on the mind as on technique, using his own mind to penetrate that of the opponent, and being so disciplined as to reveal nothing of his state of mind or his next movement. Like the moon on water or the reflection in a mirror, his mind simply reflected his opponent's, although with compassion, rather than aggression, as its base.

In 1559, Kamiizumi was introduced to the Buddhist priest In'ei of the Hozoin Temple in Nara. In'ei was skillful with a number of weapons, but he specialized in the spear and had radically improved the techniques known for fighting with this weapon. He was also a friend of the famous swordsman Yagyu Sekishusai Muneyoshi. Whether out of admiration for both Kamiizumi and Sekishusai, or from a sense of mischief, In'ei arranged for a match between the two swordsmen to be held on the same temple grounds where Miyamoto Musashi would de-feat In'ei's disciples some forty years later. Muneyoshi grasped a *bokken*, or wooden sword. His opponent in the first match, Kamiizumi's nephew Hikita Kagekane, held a sword-like weapon that Sekishusai had likely never seen before: the *fukuro shinai,* another measure of Kamiizumi's sense of compassion.

It is a specialty of the Shinkage-ryu to practice with this *fukuro shinai,* a split length of bamboo covered with a leather sheath, further developed into what is called the *hikihada* ("toad-skin") *shinai.* This is made by selecting a high-quality cow or horse hide and stiffening it by applying lacquer. The numerous wrinkles that run along the outside of the treated leather resemble the skin of a toad, and thus its name. The bamboo that is wrapped within the *hikihada* pouch for matches is split two to four times. For practice, the hilt is about seven inches long and retains the form of the bamboo. The "blade" is about twenty-nine inches long, split into a number of strips, and covered with "toadskin."

Using the *fukuro shinai,* practitioners can strike one another as though they were fighting with real swords. This is not possible with the hard wooden *bokken.* With this instrument, one must either "pull" his stroke (*tsumeru*), strike down his opponent's *bokken,* or attack the base of the "sword" guard. Since injuries can occur this way, practice is usually done in *kata,* or "forms," resulting in some lack of realism.

Sekishusai was an accomplished swordsman of both the Tomita and Shinto styles, and had a reputation in the Nara-Kyoto area as being quite formidable. At thirty-five he had experienced a number of battles and had justifiable self-confidence. Thus he was taken aback when he was quickly defeated twice, not by the master himself, but by the master's disciple Kagekane—by all accounts a man who did not have the appearance of a swordsman at all. Sekishusai felt humiliated, and so was very surprised to hear the fifty-five-year-old Kamiizumi himself next request a match with him. The two faced off, and just moments later Sekishusai dropped to his knees and admitted defeat. Yet, nothing had happened, no action had occurred. The younger man had simply stood and found no opening to make an attack. The match ended with Sekishusai's perceptive recognition of this fact.

Indeed, it was Kamiizumi's recognition of Sekishusai's perception and skill that moved him to challenge the twice-defeated swordsman. This was a man worth teaching.

Sekishusai and In'ei both requested instruction from Kamiizumi, and were granted it. Sekishusai led the older man and his two disciples back to his villa at Yagyu-mura, where they stayed for the next two years imparting the techniques, philosophy, and mysteries of the Shinkage-ryu to students. The further result of Sekishusai's request, however, was the development of the Yagyu Shinkage-ryu, the style that years later Munenori would bring to perfection and establish as the preeminent school of swordsmanship in Japan. And it was at this moment, some twelve years before he was born, that Munenori's life would be defined.

BACKGROUND

The Kizu River flows out of its tributaries to the south and west, and runs for some distance close to the border between Kyoto and Nara prefectures. A few miles before turning north toward the city of Kyoto, it comes into view of Mount Kasagi, at the southern foot of which are located a number of *kakurezato*, or hidden villages. Most villages of this type are hemmed in—or you might say, protected—on nearly all sides by low but steep mountains, and for centuries they could only be approached through narrow passes or small, obscure paths. Such entryways are quickly snowed in with the first heavy winter storms, and mountain passes and valley pathways alike are obscured to the point of being unrecognizable.

The *kakurezato* were, from early in Japan's history, near-perfect refuges for defeated samurai. Unable to return to the capital or their former fiefs, such men sought safety in these out-of-the-way places, where they often built homes and turned to farming. Many remained mindful of their origins, however, and passed the skills of their martial traditions down to the next generations. It was a fact of life in these hidden valleys that one could practice an art without distraction and without attracting too much attention.

Yagyu-mura was one such village in this area, as was Iga, the home of families skilled in espionage and covert actions, not far to the northwest. Yagyu-mura seems to have been inhabited since 645 C.E. and has always been noted for producing excellent swordsmen. The Yagyu clan traces its ancestors there back to the eleventh century. They appear to have taken the family name sometime during the Kamakura period (1192–1333), and soon took on the responsibility for supervising the village, which eventually became their private fief.

Although Yagyu-mura was a hidden village, by the sixteenth century it had been drawn into the wars and battles being waged around it. The relatively small number of troops—about a thousand men—ensconced in Koyagyu Castle were forced to fight—now for one daimyo, now for another—and sometimes had to endure being pressed into the service of larger forces that had just defeated them. Throughout this period, the smaller clans had not only to strengthen their own organization but to learn to swim among the larger military clans. In this way, swordsmanship was just a part of the martial arts of the Yagyu; the clan's survival depended on military ability, political astuteness, and even attention to the more refined arts as well.

Yagyu Mataemon Munenori was born in 1571, the youngest son among five brothers and six sisters. That same year his eldest brother, Shinjiro Yoshikatsu, while accompanying his father in battle was hit in the hip by a rifleball for the second time, and permanently crippled. The second eldest, Kyusai, and the third son, Tokusai, had already shaved their heads and become Buddhist monks, while the fourth son, Goroemon, had left the village when young and gone into the service of Kobayakawa Hideaki. Goroemon would later establish his own school of swordsmanship, but it was Munenori, the youngest, who showed the greatest promise in the art, starting his practice at a very young age. His early years in Yagyu-mura, however, were not idyllic.

After receiving the *inka* from Kamiizumi,[5] Sekishusai had hoped to devote his time to perfecting his sword style, but the chaotic events occurring around the nation and in nearby areas would not permit him to stay at his manor undisturbed. When Oda Nobunaga established Ashikaga Yoshiaki as shogun in October of 1569, Sekishusai was requested to guide twenty thousand of the great general's troops through Yamato Prefecture. In the following years Sekishusai became a sort of go-between for Nobunaga and Yoshiaki, and quickly came into great favor with the shogun. This, however, worked to his disadvantage when Nobunaga decided to destroy the shogunate and drove Yoshiaki out of Kyoto in 1573.

Sekishusai, then forty-five years old, had run back and forth between the two men and their officials for nearly five years, trying to maintain the fragile balance of power that they shared. Now, disappointed, he resigned his position, returned to Yagyu-mura, and devoted himself to unifying the Shinto, Nen, and Tomita styles into the Shinkage-ryu. He would stay away from the world as much as possible for the next twenty-one years.

In June of 1582, Nobunaga himself was betrayed and killed by one of his own generals, and power fell to Toyotomi Hideyoshi. It was Hideyoshi who, three years later, for what may have been political reasons, accused Sekishusai of hiding land from taxation, dispossessed him of most of his manor, and caused the Yagyu clan to disperse for a number of years. The fourteen-year-old

Munenori entered the service of the Hosokawa clan the following year, but in 1594, at the age of twenty-three, took leave to visit his family back at Yagyu.

Then came the invitation from Ieyasu for a meeting at his villa at Takagamine.

The demonstration of No-Sword on the outskirts of Kyoto must have impressed Ieyasu to an unusual degree, for he was not a man to make snap judgments. He had, of course, not forgotten the logistic advantages of securing the Yagyu's gratitude. But that he not only immediately wrote out a pledge to Sekishusai but also took the young Munenori with him as a personal sword instructor and retainer indicates that he perceived something of extraordinary value in both the father and son. No doubt the future shogun noted in Munenori's intellect and perspicacious manner qualities that would be assets to have close at hand, not only for himself, but for his descendants. And certainly the young man's ability in swordsmanship and especially the Yagyu art of No-Sword filled him with admiration and delight.

Very likely, Sekishusai and Munenori explained this central technique to Ieyasu in terms based on rational laws of combat rather than the mystical justifications often used to impress the uninitiated. What he said at the time we will never know, but years later Munenori would write:

> The significance of the term No-Sword is not necessarily in having to take the sword of your opponent. Neither does

it mean taking your own sword in display and making a name for yourself. No-Sword means not being cut by another, although you yourself have no sword. . . .

If your opponent does not want his sword taken, you should not insist on trying to take it. No-Sword is also in *not* taking the sword when your opponent has this attitude. A man who is consumed by the thought of not having his sword taken is going to forget the aim of cutting his opponent. When he thinks only of not having his sword taken, he will probably not cut you. . . .

What is called No-Sword is not the art of taking a man's sword; it is being able to use all implements freely. When you have no sword and wish to take your opponent's to use as your own, anything that comes into your hands should be of use. Even if you have only a fan, you should be able to defeat your opponent's sword. No-Sword is just this attitude.

One can imagine the satisfaction with which Ieyasu listened to this kind of talk that afternoon.

MILITARY SERVICE

Ieyasu was at this time assisting in the construction of Fushimi Castle, on Toyotomi Hideyoshi's orders, and had made Takagamine his field camp. During the next few years, Munenori was very often close at Ieyasu's side as his personal trusted retainer, and thus at the nucleus of what would become the Tokugawa *bakufu*, or government. He was teaching Ieyasu the Shinkage-ryu school of swordsmanship and fast becoming known as a "living master of the sword." The insights he had gained from Sekishusai and from his own experience in political survival were augmented daily by what he observed of Ieyasu's activities, and it was evidence of Munenori's genius that he did not categorize these lessons as fundamentally distinct from swordsmanship itself. To Munenori, principles that applied to the art of civil administration applied as well to personal conflict in the martial arts and could be extended to the movement of large armies as well.

By the end of 1598, it had become clear that large armies might soon be engaged in conflict. On September 15th of that year, Hideyoshi passed away at the age of sixty-two in his palace at Fushimi. His son, Hideyori, was barely five years old at the time, and in order to secure his succession, Hideyoshi had created during his own final illness a group of five *tairo*, or chief elders, to govern Japan during the boy's minority. These men were Maeda Toshiie, Uesugi Kagekatsu, Mori Terumoto, Ukita Hideie, and the daimyo whom Hideyoshi had treated perhaps the most generously, Tokugawa Ieyasu.

Ieyasu wasted little time, and by October of 1600, he challenged the forces loyal to the Toyotomi at the plain of Sekigahara.

Munenori did not simply sit at Ieyasu's side during this battle, nor were the Yagyu to remain outside of the action. The

Battle of Sekigahara would decide the direction of the history of Japan and the fate of the Tokugawa clan, and Ieyasu would use every player he had carefully chosen over the last several years. One of the fruits of the meeting at Takagamine six years earlier would now ripen.

A few days before the opening of major hostilities, Munenori was sent by Ieyasu with a message to Sekishusai, commanding him to rally the lords of Yamato Province and disturb the enemy forces as they moved toward the battlefield. It is also conjectured that Sekishusai was to contact his in-laws and their neighbors in nearby Iga and Koga to ask them to act as undercover agents, gaining information through surveillance and causing the enemy as much trouble as possible as the enemy proceeded to its engagement with the Tokugawa armies. He may also have asked them to make contact with lords on the Toyotomi side who were beginning to think twice—a difficult job, given the high security in place everywhere.

A case in point was the young lord Kobayakawa Hideaki, once a favorite of Hideyoshi and then passed over in favor of the latter's new son. Hideaki was a linchpin of the battle at Sekigahara, and his loyalties were not clearly known. His personal sword instructor and retainer, however, was one Yagyu Goroemon Munetoshi, an elder brother of Munenori. Was there secret communication between Munenori and Munetoshi as to how, when, or even *if* to strike at the Toyotomi? Unfortunately, it is the nature of covert activities to leave no traces that might uncover the answers to this kind of question.

In the midst of the confusion, hostilities opened—not at the center of the battle lines, but on the fringes of Sekigahara. Munenori had led some troops in his father's place and met with Ieyasu's messenger at a place known as Chiryu. The day before the battle, he greeted Ieyasu at Yoshigoe and joined the forces under Ieyasu's command. On the day of the battle, when the Toyotomi samurai pushed close to Ieyasu's main body of troops, Munenori fought with courage, cutting down eight enemy soldiers and driving others into retreat. This success certainly did not go unnoticed by Ieyasu, and he would likely relate the story to his son Hidetada for the son's benefit.

There is in fact almost no documentation as to what transpired beyond the battlefield before these events, but it would seem that the now-adult Munenori developed stronger relations with the ninja families of his local area throughout this period, and that these same families gained the gratitude and trust of the man who would soon become shogun. What *is* documented, however, is that for whatever services Munenori and Sekishusai rendered on and off the battlefield, soon after the devastating defeat of the Toyotomi, Ieyasu awarded the Yagyu the two-thousand-*koku* fief formerly taken from them by Hideyoshi,[6] and a year later added yet another thousand. In addition, Munenori was appointed to the position of *hatamoto*, or direct vassal to the shogun.

That same year Munenori was commanded to be the sword instructor to Ieyasu's son, Hidetada, who was by most accounts an indifferent student at best. Munenori, however, impressed Hidetada, not only with his swordsmanship, but with his emphasis on the art as a vehicle for inner development rather than simply for killing. With this approach, he contrasted favorably in Hidetada's mind with the shogun's other sword instructor, Ono no Tadaaki of the Itto-ryu, who was overbearing and severe, and carried his reputation for cruelty almost proudly. Munenori no doubt took Hidetada's character into account, and taught him appropriately. Tadaaki, on the other hand, likely saw the young Tokugawa simply as a vehicle for his own techniques.

Whatever dynamics were at play here, in 1605, when Hidetada became the second Tokugawa shogun, the Yagyu Shinkage-ryu was established as the shogun's official school of swordsmanship, and was considered the true art of the sword that would rule the country in peace.

In 1606, after a lifetime of dedication to the art of swordsmanship, Sekishusai passed away in Yagyu-mura at the age of seventy-seven. Munenori had now been with the Tokugawa for twelve years, and questions have sometimes been raised as to how much Sekishusai had approved of his son's remaining in the bustling new city of Edo and whether he approved of Munenori's increasing involvement in political life. Surely he was proud of his son's achievements and felt assured in the security of his clan's future. But Sekishusai's life had long been centered on the art of the sword, in all its physical and spiritual dimensions, and he may have wondered if Munenori was being sidetracked by the allure of power and prestige as a result of being in such close proximity to the shogun and his family. He may also have wondered about Munenori's overriding interest in Zen Buddhism.

It is interesting in this regard that upon his death, Sekishusai passed the title of head of family on to Munenori, due to his reasonable confidence that the clan would continue under shogunal protection. But he passed the *inka* and secret written materials he had received from Kamiizumi on to his grandson, Yagyu Hyogonosuke Toshiyoshi (1577–1650), the son of his eldest son, Shinjiro Yoshikatsu, who had been wounded and crippled so many years before. This established Hyogonosuke as successor to the leadership of the Yagyu Shinkage-ryu. Hyogonosuke was said to be closest in character and ability to his grandfather, and was indeed a favorite among family members. He eventually went to Owari (Nagoya) and became sword instructor to Tokugawa Yoshinao, Ieyasu's seventh son; and it is his Owari Yagyu Shinkage-ryu that continues in lineage to the twenty-first grand master today.

Hyogonosuke studied both Zen and Mikkyo, or esoteric Buddhism, and was said to have had an approachable and friendly character. He was known to be the apple of his grandfather's eye and greatly beloved by his great-grandfather, Mimasaka Nyudo Ieyoshi. It was Hyogonosuke who spent an afternoon talking and playing the game of go with itinerant swordsman Miyamoto

Musashi, and tradition has it that the two of them worked out new sword techniques together. Sadly, no such meeting ever took place between Musashi and Munenori.

Munenori continued as teacher and advisor to the shogun, and was increasingly well regarded by the Tokugawa family and those in their immediate circle. His keen perception of the men around him made him a valuable counselor to Hidetada, and his earlier contacts with experts in espionage may have made him a convenient source of information on events and trends around the country. And, as he had demonstrated by his actions at Osaka Castle in 1615, his abilities clearly extended beyond the dojo and the politics in Edo.

THE THIRD SHOGUN

Munenori had served the first two Tokugawa shoguns from the time he was young, and in the fall of 1620, at the age of forty-nine, he became instructor and tutor to Hidetada's son Iemitsu, who was then just seventeen. In 1621, Iemitsu signed a pledge with Munenori much like the one made at Takagamine. In 1623, Iemitsu became shogun at the age of twenty, and Munenori's life would never be the same.

Despite his young age, or perhaps because of it, Iemitsu was self-confident and high-handed. But he was also intelligent and extraordinarily determined to be in full control. He demonstrated little sense of restraint and was, according to a contemporary cleric, a man not easily approachable. He was also an avid swordsman and very demanding of his teacher.

With his work as instructor of the martial arts, his position as head of the Yagyu clan, and his responsibilities to the shoguns, Munenori had never had a great amount of time for himself, but now he was to have even less. It would seem that he now became a sort of foster father to the young shogun, and that this relationship would endure. Munenori not only tutored the young Iemitsu in swordsmanship but also advised him on politics and accompanied him to performances of Noh drama, martial arts exhibitions, and tea ceremonies. He further had the duty of being at Iemitsu's side during conferences with the other daimyo. These duties, however, were not without their rewards.

In March of 1629, Munenori was promoted to Junior Fifth Rank and took the title of Tajima no kami. Three years later, at age sixty-two, he was appointed to the post of *sometsuke*, or Inspector-General; this meant that he, in addition to his many other duties, was to keep a close eye on the activities of the various daimyo. He served in this post for seven years. To Iemitsu, it was no doubt a perfectly appropriate position for someone with an extensive intelligence background and connections beyond the normal flow of public information.

With these promotions, Munenori's stipend was progressively

increased until, in 1633, he was promoted to the rank of daimyo with a fief of ten thousand *koku*. Eventually he would reach a position that brought him twelve thousand five hundred *koku*, a stipend unimaginable for a sword instructor.

Iemitsu relied in some way on Munenori for nearly every aspect of his life, and Munenori was generously compensated. But Iemitsu was not an easy student and he may have been a difficult companion. With so much of his life defined by domestic governmental matters, religious controversies, the threat of foreign influences, and the practice of other polite arts expected of people in the upper echelons of society, Iemitsu likely had less time for practice in the dojo than he would have liked. This was not a satisfactory situation for a man known for his impatience.

In 1630, Munenori issued a document to the shogun, certifying that he had been initiated into the secrets of the Yagyu Shinkage-ryu of swordsmanship; in return he was promoted in rank and presented with a sword made by the renowned smith Masamune. Not long after receiving this certificate, however, Iemitsu sent Munenori a now-famous letter—almost threatening in tone—accusing his instructor of not teaching him to the fullest. Again, this may indicate Iemitsu's frustration at his own lack of progress or that he was simply taking advantage of his position and trying to push Munenori to new limits. No matter what the reason, Iemitsu would continue to entreat Munenori for further sword instruction, importuning him until the old teacher's dying day.

THE BUDDHIST PRIEST

> I write this down as the instructions I received from a Buddhist priest.
>
> *Heiho kadensho*

It will perhaps not be going too far to declare that the philosophical and psychological foundation of the Yagyu Shinkage-ryu as taught by Munenori is Zen Buddhism. Zen permeates Munenori's explanations of the correct mental attitudes for swordsmanship, and he very often quotes the old Zen masters and Zen literature to aid or deepen the student's understanding. His approach is not exactly a validation of techniques by the use of Zen concepts, but it is close to that, and the value he placed on those concepts cannot be overstated.

Munenori would surely have been exposed to Zen Buddhism during childhood by his father Sekishusai and in the course of his normal religious upbringing. Sekishusai, however, seems to have made a very even assessment of Zen, incorporating it into his own art but leaving few obvious traces. An eclectic, he may have studied other kinds of Buddhism as well, notably Mikkyo,[7] the esoteric sects.

It is difficult to say when Munenori first met Takuan Soho, the man who would influence his life so much with Zen. The agents of this contact may have been the Hosokawa, who had a long relationship with Takuan, and to whom Munenori was attached during his late teens and early twenties. But almost nothing of this is known. What is certain is that over the years,

Munenori and Takuan would become close friends and associates, that Takuan would have an extraordinary influence on Munenori's thought in regard to his own art, and that eventually Iemitsu would be drawn into the circle and come to rely on Takuan's advice as well.

Takuan Soho was born into a samurai family in the town of Izushi, province of Tajima (now part of Hyogo Prefecture), in 1573. He began studying Jodo, or Pure Land Buddhism, at age ten, but converted to the Rinzai Zen sect at the age of fourteen. Takuan was a polymath, and was not only one of the most accomplished and sought-after Zen monks of his day, but a calligrapher, painter, poet, gardener, and tea master. He was also quite happy to play in the kitchen, where he invented the pickle named after him—ubiquitous on Japanese tables even today. His collected writings fill six volumes.

In 1608, Takuan became the fifty-fourth chief priest of the Daitokuji—one of the major Zen temples in Kyoto—but he resigned after three days and returned to a small temple in his hometown. This might be taken as an indication of his character, his lack of interest in power and authority, and his independence from the world at large. "If you follow the present-day world," he wrote, "you will turn your back on the Way. If you would not turn your back on the Way, do not follow the world."

Nevertheless, when the Tokugawa government established a system of edicts known as *jiin shohatto*, placing all temples and ecclesiastic promotions under the oversight of the shogunate, Takuan protested publicly in 1628 and the following year was exiled to the city of Kaminomiya in the far north province of Dewa. Here he was placed under the watchful but likely appreciative eye of a Lord Matsudaira. And here he may have learned something more of swordsmanship from Miyamoto Musashi, who was in the area in 1631 demonstrating his sword style to Lord Matsudaira Dewa no kami. In 1632, Takuan was pardoned as part of an amnesty upon the death of the second Tokugawa shogun, Hidetada. This pardon resulted partly from the intercession of Munenori—who had known Takuan for some time—and a number of other notables, including Takuan's friend the emperor, Go-Mizuno, to whom he had taught Zen.

Soon afterward Takuan wrote the *Fudochi shinmyoroku* for Munenori, to explain the connection between Zen and the martial arts. If this would seem to be an obsequious gesture to his swordsman benefactor, however, it should be noted that the closing paragraphs of the work criticize Munenori severely for everything from his child-rearing techniques to his pride in his abilities in Noh. Nevertheless, this short essay so strongly influenced Munenori's view of his own art that he both quoted and paraphrased it in his own work, *Heiho kadensho*.

In 1634, an event occurred that was curiously parallel to Munenori's meeting with Ieyasu forty years earlier: Iemitsu visited Kyoto, and Takuan was persuaded by Munenori to pay the shogun a courtesy call. Munenori knew Iemitsu's character quite well by this time, and the outcome of the meeting was as Munenori might have predicted: Iemitsu was completely captivated by Takuan's character and, despite the latter's own desires, ordered him to Edo. There the shogun eventually built a temple—the Tokaiji—for Takuan, to keep him available for the shogun's own needs. Thus, Takuan became a frequent advisor to Iemitsu and a more frequent companion to Munenori. One imagines Munenori's quiet satisfaction with these circumstances, and the happiness and mental stimulation that Takuan must have provided him as the two grew older.

Takuan remained in Edo for the remainder of his life and passed away in December of 1645 at the age of seventy-three.

Takuan's forcefulness and uncompromising individuality are apparent in both his writings and his calligraphy, an interesting and famous example of which was his very last. As death approached, he instructed his disciples:

> Bury my body in the mountain behind the temple, cover it with dirt, and go home. Read no sutras, and hold no ceremony. Receive no gifts from either monk or laity. Let the monks wear their robes, eat their meals, and carry on as on normal days.

Pressed by those in attendance for a death poem at his final moment, he wrote the Chinese character for dream,[8] put down the brush, and died.

It may be said that Munenori's greatest monument to Takuan and the *Fudochi shinmyoroku* was his own written classic, the *Heiho kadensho*. For although he signed it with the names of Kamiizumi and the Yagyu father and son, throughout the work we can almost sense Munenori waiting for an approving "Kwatz!"[9] from the eccentric old priest.

THE LIFE-GIVING SWORD (HEIHO KADENSHO)

Schools of the martial arts began to proliferate during the latter part of the Muromachi period (1336–1568), and many of these claimed inspiration or protection from the gods, Buddhas, and other supernatural sources. Thus they were able to lay claim to transcendental energy, mysterious techniques, and sources beyond ordinary human powers. Tsukahara Bokuden of the Shinto-ryu, for example, received a "divine decree" at the Kashima Shrine; and the founder of the Itto-ryu, Ito Ittosai, had his style revealed to him after seven days and seven nights' seclusion at the Grand Shrine at Mishima. Okayama Kyugasai's eyes were opened to the Shinkage-ryu (in this case, written with different characters)[10] by the gracious deity of Mikawa Okuyama; Jion of the Nen-ryu was enlightened to the secrets of his style at the Kurama Temple in Kyoto; Hayashizaki Jinsuke, the restorer of *iaido*, discovered his new Way at the Dewa Tateoka Hayashizaki Shrine; and Fukui Hei' emon received the principles of the Shindo Munen-ryu from the deity Izuna Gongen in Shinshu.

Styles that emphasized such supernatural origins and resultant near-magical abilities, however, eventually began to explain their techniques from a more reasonable standpoint, in time graduating to the principles of psychology. Thus, rather than being enlightened by the authority of a spirit, one grasped the principles of swordsmanship by means of his own discipline and depth of true understanding.

The Yagyu Shinkage-ryu was representative of this trend, and it was Yagyu Munenori—inheriting the techniques of Matsumoto, Ikosai, Kamiizumi and Sekishusai—who deepened and organized the system of psychology and technique in this school.

This system was recorded by Munenori in *Heiho kadensho* in 1632 or soon thereafter. The work is in part a catalog of the Yagyu clan's techniques and in part an explanation of the underlying principles of those techniques. So it is at once a prompt or reference guide, a book of carefully worded instructions for practice, a meditative source for eliminating psychological problems, and a philosophical basis for using the sword as an instrument of life rather than death.

Finally, it was in the teaching of Takuan Soho that Munenori was able to introduce Zen philosophy into the martial arts and confirm the concept of *kenzen ichinyo*, or the "sameness of sword and Zen."[11] This concept was emphasized in *Fudochi shinmyoroku* as Takuan explained one of the basic intersections of Zen and swordsmanship:

There are many instances where the martial arts and Buddhism are in accordance, and where the martial arts can be understood through Zen. Both especially abhor attachment and stopping at things. . . . No matter what kind of secret tradition you may inherit or what kind of technique you use, if the mind stops at that technique, you will lose in the martial arts. Regardless of your opponent's actions, cutting or thrusting, it is an essential discipline that the mind does not stop at such a place.

Takuan's underlying advice was for the swordsman to cast away all attachment, become enlightened, and establish himself in No-Mind. If he did so, both body and sword would move naturally, and he would exhibit, without self-consciousness, both spirit and technique in those movements.

Heiho kadensho is divided into three chapters: "The Shoe-Presenting Bridge," which is basically a catalog of techniques that was presented to the student as certification that he had vigorously studied those techniques; "The Death-Dealing Sword," which goes into some depth about techniques and begins to explain the psychology of the school; and "The Life-Giving Sword," which continues to discuss both technique and psychology and which ends with a section on the central technique of the Yagyu Shinkage-ryu, the No-Sword.

It should be noted that there are several different levels to the concepts of the Death-Dealing Sword and the Life-Giving Sword. Munenori (and Takuan) presented these terms philosophically in keeping with what their words suggest: the sword can be used to kill, but can also be used to preserve or give life. In the latter case, a swordsman should be able to subdue an opponent without killing him, or may have to kill an evil swordsman and thereby save (give life to) countless others. This is one example of how Munenori's swordsmanship is not meant to be separated from his politics, and can thus be studied as a way of life.

In regard to pure technique, however, the difference between the two should be understood in a slightly different light. The Death-Dealing Sword is one that meets an opponent head-on in a sense, by overcoming or stifling his technique. It, in essence, "kills" the opponent's sword. The Life-Giving Sword, on the other hand, encourages or leads the opponent to begin a technique—and thus "gives life" to his sword. Then, if possible, it takes that sword away or defeats the opponent in some other way. This is taking the "initiating initiative" as defined in the *Tsuki no sho* and, again, is not to be understood as being applicable only to swordsmanship.

> The mind is the foundation of all thoughts, so the mind is initial. The mind is prior. The very first thought is the initial act. Therefore it is the initiating initiative. This is the ultimate. The very first thought is the foundation of all acts.

There are a few basic concepts emphasized in *Heiho kadensho* that bear noting before reading the text. These are the basic building blocks upon which Munenori supports his style, and without which the disciple might become skilled, but not truly accomplished, regardless of his own natural abilities.

The first is the attitude taken toward training itself. Munenori stressed that practice, or training in technique, is done in order to transcend technique altogether. It is by taking training to its very ultimate that the swordsman removes himself from it and goes beyond the fetters that training, technique, or any practice can become. Disciplined training internalizes the practice to the point that it becomes completely natural and can be executed with no interference from the mind. This brings the practitioner to the realm of *muga*, or No-Self.[12] Munenori writes:

> If you exhaustively repeat the various practices, and accumulate merit in your discipline in practice and training, the action will be in your body and limbs, and not in your mind. Distancing yourself from practice, you will not run counter to it, and you will perform every technique with freedom. At this point you will not know where your mind is, and neither demons nor heresies will be able to find it. . . .
>
> These are practices for reaching the stage of *muga*. If you are able to make them your own, they will disappear. This is the ultimate meaning of all Ways.

Whether the student practices swordsmanship, archery, calligraphy, or tea ceremony, any conscious understanding of the practice that remains in the mind will only cause conflict during a performance. Ultimately, the student must practice and practice with such profound concentration that practice ceases to exist altogether.

Munenori approached the same point from a slightly different angle in his discussion of "sickness," and as before, he placed the emphasis on the mind. Again, whatever remains in the mind becomes a hindrance to freedom or to "free and easy movement." This applies directly to the understanding one should have of a sword match:

> To think only of winning is sickness. To think only of using the martial arts is sickness. To think only of demonstrating the results of one's training is sickness, as is thinking only of making an attack or waiting for one. To think in a fixated way only of expelling such sickness is also sickness. *Whatever remains absolutely in the mind should be considered sickness* [italics added].

Although intended mainly to apply to one-on-one matches with swords, such concepts can be understood as relating to many situations; in this sense Munenori's mind moved among various arenas simultaneously—from swordsmanship to political administration to the daily living of one's life.

Another concept related to Munenori's style is that of Emptiness. For him, Emptiness is an understanding rather than a concept and in fact it transcends conceptual thinking. With an intuitive understanding of Emptiness, a swordsman is able to see the existent and the non-existent, the inside and the outside, and the active and pre-active. Thus he is able to judge his opponent's moves and tactics while they are still below the surface, not yet manifested in action. Such abilities require intense concentration, disciplined meditation, and proper instruction but, according to Munenori, can be achieved.

This is not some mystical mumbo-jumbo, but a way of thinking supported by Zen Buddhist philosophy (which tends toward the practical) and confirmed by Munenori's history. Problems arise, of course, when we apply words to nonconceptual understandings; perhaps this is why the literature of Zen Buddhism often seems to be filled with paradoxes and non sequiturs. Ordinarily language seems to fail here, but one must try. Munenori takes several different tacks in an effort to work around this problem in *Heiho kadensho*, but then informs us with certainty:

> "Emptiness" means the mind of your opponent. The mind has no form and no color, and is void. The phrase "to see Emptiness, the One Alone" refers to seeing the mind of your opponent. Buddhism enlightens you to the fact that this mind is Emptiness.

And,

> Your opponent's mind is in his hands and is being held

up, or consecrated [that is, concentrated], there. Striking at the place that does not move is called "Striking at Emptiness." Emptiness does not move, because it has no form. The significance of striking at Emptiness is that you strike at the place that does not move. This is called Emptiness, and it is the fundamental principle of Buddhism.

In other sections of *Heiho kadensho*, the vocabulary is not quite so easily understood, and it is typical of Munenori to use specialized terms from Zen and Confucian philosophy. This is interesting on a number of levels, not the least of which is that it indicates a high level of education among the sword practitioners taught by Munenori and his designated instructors. The reader is encouraged to be patient with these unfamiliar terms. Repeated reading of the book—clearly a practice in itself—will likely result in a familiarity leading to an intuitive understanding.

The breadth of Munenori's education is apparent throughout *Heiho kadensho*, with his numerous quotes from Buddhist and Chinese literature. His admiration for Takuan, who may have instructed or at least led him in his intellectual pursuits, is evident from even a superficial reading of the book, but it becomes even clearer from a side-by-side reading of *Fudochi shinmyoroku*. It is a measure of Munenori's genius that he was able to substantiate his sword style and strengthen his readers' understanding with perfect examples from the Zen classics, and a measure of his earnestness and his good fortune to have had an advisor and friend in Takuan.

Munenori's philosophy and psychology as recorded in *Heiho kadensho* reach farther than swordsmanship or even the martial arts. As Munenori himself wrote, it recognizes the martial arts in many aspects of our lives:

> Having no conflicts in association with friends from beginning to end is also a matter of seeing into the principles of a relationship, and this, too, is a martial art of the mind. . . .
>
> Arranging objects in your living room is a matter of using what is right for each place, and this, too, is a matter of seeing into the principle of these places. This is not unlike the very heart of the martial arts. Truly, the arena may change, but the principle is the same, and thus you could even apply this to national affairs and make no mistakes. . . .
>
> It is missing the point to think that the martial art is solely in cutting a man down.

Munenori hoped to keep this essential book within the guardianship of his own school, in part so that misunderstandings would not arise about its content. But this was not to be. Circulation of the work seems to have extended beyond his school relatively early; judging from the introduction to *The Book of Five Rings*, Miyamoto Musashi had access to it in faraway Kyushu less than fifteen years after its writing. It has rightly been considered a treasure of the martial arts world ever since.

FINAL YEARS

By 1639, Munenori had become a daimyo, a remarkable achievement in light of his comparatively humble origins, and performed the duties of *sometsuke* (now termed *ometsuke*) for seven years. When he had reached his mid-sixties, he was ready to retire.

Munenori continued to deal with his responsibilities as head of the Yagyu clan, master of the Yagyu Shinkage-ryu, and general advisor and sword instructor to the shogun Iemitsu. As noted, he seems to have had very little leisure time, and he was constantly importuned by the shogun to teach him an extra lesson in swordsmanship or accompany him to one entertainment or another. Iemitsu thought nothing of dropping in on Munenori's detached villa while out hawking, or of sending a palanquin to his old teacher's residence and having him brought to Edo Palace on one pretext or another.

In May of 1645, Munenori was seventy-five years old, and requested permission to return for a time to Yagyu-mura. After so many years of service to three shoguns in Edo, this was a petition that not even Iemitsu could refuse—although he would not grant it, of course, until he had had a few more lectures on the secret principles of swordsmanship.

It is difficult to imagine Munenori's thoughts upon coming—for what might prove the last time—out of the narrow paths that led into the hidden valley. This was the place of his birth and early childhood, and the very place where Kamiizumi Ise no kami Hidetsuna had taught his style to Sekishusai and left him with the challenge of perfecting the art of No-Sword. What were his feelings as he contemplated the quiet fields and surrounding mountains? What kind of life had he left behind for fifty years while living in the new capital?

Munenori stayed in Yagyu-mura through the summer and early winter, watching the deepening green of the foliage, the rice harvest, and the turning of the autumn leaves. But after the first few snows, he finally returned to Edo. On his arrival, he suddenly became ill, and seemed to understand that he would not recover. He had not, in all his life, been sick for more than three days.

Upon being informed that Munenori's illness was serious, Iemitsu himself went to visit the Yagyu detached villa in Higakubo, on the third of February. Alarmed by his teacher's condition, he sent an express messenger three days later to summon the famous doctor Takeda Doan from Kyoto. On the 20th of the month, he went to visit the ailing Munenori once again. This time, the old swordsman who had been so robust all his life needed assistance in order to greet the shogun in a proper way. True to form, Iemitsu dismissed the attendants, and then asked once again if Munenori had any remaining secret principles of swordsmanship to impart. Assured that his instructor had held nothing back from him, he then inquired if Munenori had any last requests. True to his own character, Munenori commended his sons, Jubei Mitsuyoshi and Matajuro Munefuyu, to the shogun's patronage, and then requested that a monument be built to his father Sekishusai at the Yagyu manor. Iemitsu did not hes- itate to agree.

On 25 March 1646, physician Takeda Doan finally arrived from Kyoto, but nothing more could be done. Munenori passed away peacefully the next day, at the age of seventy-six. On 6 April, his ashes were placed at the Kotoku Temple in the Shimodani section of Edo.

Munenori had been preceded in death by the swordsman Miyamoto Musashi, who died on 19 May 1645, and by Takuan Soho, who passed away in December the same year. Iemitsu, who after Munenori's final illness was sometimes heard to say, "If only Munenori were here, I could ask him about this," lived on until 20 April 1651.

MUNENORI'S CHARACTER

Munenori was just fourteen years old when the lands possessed by the Yagyu manor were confiscated by the Toyotomi in 1585, and his family scattered in the four directions. Although he would become attached to the powerful Hosokawa forces only two years later, he must have watched with anxiety as his father and the rest of the family struggled in poverty and hardship for the next eight years. The Yagyu had never been more than well-established gentry whose domain was limited to the hid- den valley containing Yagyu-mura and the Old Yagyu Castle. Even as a child, Munenori would have observed Sekishusai's maneuvering among the larger clans—allying himself now with one, now with another—in order to survive.

Moreover, Munenori knew that, with the crippling of his eldest brother, two other elder brothers becoming Buddhist priests, and his only other brother firmly attached to another clan, the responsibility of caring for the Yagyu would eventually be set squarely on his shoulders. To seal this fate, he seemed to have an extraordinary talent in swordsmanship, the art of his father.

In this way, Munenori likely developed a healthy respect for the problem of survival and a keen awareness of political reality early on. His connections with his uncles and their families in Iga too would have given him an understanding of currents not always obvious to others, and provided him with another dimension to his comprehension of the constant interplay of the existent and non-existent, the hidden and the manifest.

This combination of sensitivity to and personal interest in the visible and unseen tides of politics imparted a thoughtful character to the man. His serious nature would only be deepened by his relationship with three successive shoguns who relied on him, each more than the one before, for everything from swordsmanship to politics to his understanding of literature.

While the Tokugawa annals report mainly Munenori's comings and goings, there are several well-known anecdotes that reveal Munenori's awareness and powers of observation, in addition to his political acumen.

In 1637, for example, when the Shimabara rebellion broke out in Kyushu, a certain Itakura Shigemasa was appointed to lead the forces against the rebels and was quickly sent off to the field of battle far to the southwest. When Munenori learned of this development a short time later, he wasted no time in appealing to higher authorities, but went himself on horseback in pursuit of Shigemasa, riding late into the night. Realizing that he was too late to catch up to the man, Munenori returned to Edo and appealed directly to Iemitsu to rescind the order for Shigemasa's post. Iemitsu was not one to have his appointments questioned, however, and stalked from the room.

The following morning, the shogun was informed that Munenori had waited unmoving through the night and was still seated where Iemitsu had left him. Rejoining his old teacher and asking the reason for this stubborn behavior, Iemitsu was informed by Munenori that, although Shigemasa was a splendid warrior and loyal to the shogunate, his relatively low status would cause the Kyushu daimyo to disregard his authority, and that this in the end would result in Shigemasa's death. Iemitsu listened patiently but would not reverse his order. By the end of the year, however, when the situation had progressed as Munenori predicted and Shigemasa's authority had been undermined, a new commander was chosen to replace him. On 1 January 1638, upon hearing that he would soon be replaced, Shigemasa led a last, desperate attack on the rebel castle and was shot and killed.

This story reveals not only Munenori's understanding of

the subtleties of military strategy and diplomacy, but his self-assurance, perseverance, and loyalty. It may also indicate something of the underground lines of information to which Munenori was privy. We can see Munenori sitting patiently alone throughout the night, ever the teacher, even in the most unrewarding situations.

It is said that after this event, Iemitsu relied on Munenori's advice more heavily than ever.

Yet another anecdote gives us a sense of Munenori's acuity of perception, but also hints at a sense of humor he may ordinarily have held in check. It also seems to reveal as much about the other participants as about Munenori.

Munenori was once invited by Iemitsu to attend a Noh performance given by Kanze Sakon, and was asked to sit next to the shogun. Just before the performance, Iemitsu ordered Munenori to watch Kanze's actions carefully, and to inform him later if there was any point during the acting when Kanze's attention was distracted enough that Munenori might be able to attack him. Throughout Kanze's dance, his attention was so complete that the shogun felt certain that even the master swordsman could find no opening.

Finally, Kanze finished the dance and entered the dressing room, dripping with sweat. "Today," he said, "there was someone sitting next to his lordship who never took his eyes off my performance, even for a second. Who was that?" When his attendant replied that it was Yagyu Munenori, Kanze forced a little smile and said, "Is that so? His eyes were following me all along, so I continued to dance, hardly daring to breathe. But when I finally passed the stage right pillar, I stopped for a breath and he gave a little smile. Really, I was mentally exhausted!"

After seeing Kanze off and leaving the theater, Iemitsu asked Munenori if there had been a moment when he might have attacked Kanze and struck him down. "Well," Munenori replied, "Kanze left no opening during the entire dance, but just as he passed the pillar he let out a gasp. There I could have cut him down with no difficulty." Not long after this event, both Kanze and Munenori were informed of the other's words, and each was impressed at the other's ability.

In the spring of 1630, Munenori wrote to his disciple, Kimura Sukekuro:

> There is a principle in every step, in every look. This is the mentality of the Konparu school of Noh. It is also the truth in the martial arts, and so this is quite interesting.

Munenori's interest in Noh—especially its dance—and the other arts was not simply a matter of enjoyment. He also understood that mysterious truth—that with one Way, a man could understand all Ways.

Yet Munenori may have enjoyed Noh for his own pleasure as well. No less a person than Takuan criticized him for his pride in this art and even accused him of showing off in front of the other daimyo.[13] There can be no doubt that Munenori took his old friend's admonishment to heart.

Another anecdote also reveals a number of things about the man. One afternoon in spring, later in Munenori's life, he sat on his veranda, completely engrossed in the full bloom of the cherry blossoms. Suddenly intuiting a danger behind him, he swung around to look. To his surprise, only the page in charge of holding his master's sheathed sword knelt quietly behind him. Nothing was amiss. This incident depressed Munenori, as he had dedicated his life to sharpening his senses to danger and unspoken threat. Noticing his master's darkened mood, the page inquired as to the cause. At Munenori's explanation, the page bowed deeply, apologized, and confessed that at watching his master's abstraction in the spring scene, he had wondered for just a moment if even a swordsman as accomplished as Yagyu Munenori might be attacked and killed while so absorbed. Munenori is said to have been quite satisfied with this revelation, never mentioning the matter again.

Munenori, then, was quite human, and had at least a few human frailties. An indication of this can be seen in the postscript to the *Fudochi shinmyoroku*, where Takuan takes his friend to task on a number of accounts, especially concerning Munenori's son Jubei Mitsuyoshi:

Above all, concerning your honored son's behavior, it is going at things backwards to attack a child's wrongdoings if the parent himself is incorrect. If you will first make your own conduct correct and then voice your opinions, not only will the child naturally correct himself, but his younger brother will learn from his conduct and become correct himself.

We are not told what this "incorrect" conduct is, but Takuan goes on to imply that Munenori may have taken bribes from various daimyo and sometimes neglected his "right-mindedness."

Nevertheless, Munenori was honored among the daimyo, sought out as a teacher of swordsmanship, and advanced to a station far beyond that of other sword masters of the time. If he was naturally held in some apprehension by others due to his position as *sometsuke* and his proximity to the shogun, there is no evidence that he was disliked or feared outright. And if in fact he had a slight tendency to show off his learning—as is indicated by the sheer number of quotes in *Heiho kadensho*—or his abilities in Noh performance, he no doubt fought against this weakness.

Indeed, for all of Munenori's virtues, we may well allow him his few tellurian foibles. All in all, he seems to have been a remarkably gifted, intense, and upright man who was, into the bargain, a congenial companion. Thus, it is easy to imagine what was likely an occasional scene at the shogun's palace late at night: three friends together in an intimate room removed from all disturbances: Takuan sampling the food and inappropriately testing the sake, Munenori holding forth on some current philosophical topic, and Iemitsu sitting back in bemused wonder at the great good fortune of being alive in such a world.

—WILLIAM SCOTT WILSON

THE
LIFE-GIVING
SWORD

Heiho kadensho

YAGYU MUNENORI

THE SHOE-PRESENTING BRIDGE[1]

THE BOOK OF THE SHINKAGE-RYU MARTIAL ARTS

THE THREE LEARNINGS[2]

- Stance
- Hands and Feet
- Sword

You should begin your studies with these three categories, and thus enter the gate of initial learning.

In connection with the Three Learnings, there are another Five Practices.[3]

- You should hold your body so as to present only one side to your opponent.
- Your shoulder should be on a plane with your opponent's fists.
- You should make a shield of your own fists.

- You should extend your left arm.
- Your forward knee should carry the weight of your body and the rear knee should be extended.

The very beginning of the Three Learnings is in the stances.

The very beginning is a stance with the sword, and it is called The Wheel. It is so named because you move your weapon in a circular pattern. Assume a side stance. Allowing your opponent to cut at your left shoulder, defeat him by rotating your sword in accordance with his cutting action. You should keep your stance low. At all times, be sure that your stance keeps you from being cut by your opponent. Both the construction of castles and the digging of moats are executed with the intention of preventing opponents from drawing near. So this is not a matter of cutting down your opponent. Do not make haste. Rather, make your stance fully, and do not allow yourself to be cut by your opponent.

Among priorities, the stance is considered first.

- One Cut, Two Halves[4]
- Cutting Through Nails, Slicing Through Steel
- Half-Open, Half-Opposed
- Circling Right, Turning Left
- Long and Short, One and the Same

Learning each of the above techniques is done by oral transmission; they are difficult to express in written words alone.[5]

THE NINE ITEMS[6]

- Certain Victory
- Crosswind
- Cross-Shaped Swords
- Reconciliation
- Shortcut
- Fine Stifling
- Broad Stifling
- Eight-Layered Fence
- Billowing Clouds

The above are taught by the teacher while sparring with the student. They are difficult to express on paper.

TENGU'S SELECTION: EIGHT SWORD TECHNIQUES[7]

- Flower Wheel
- Open Body
- Appropriate Waiting
- Leading
- Riotous Swords
- Preface
- Breach
- Dispatch

In addition, there are Six Techniques.[8]

- Concomitant Cutting

- Riotous Cutting
- Secret Principle
- Matchless Sword
- Life-Giving Sword
- Sword of Mystery[9]

By learning all of these techniques well and making them your own, you should develop a myriad others. The Three Learnings, the Nine Items and such, we call the basics. Once you have truly grasped this Way, you should not speak of the various sword techniques.

Devising stratagems within the closed camp curtains,[10] *victory is determined a thousand miles away.*[11]

The meaning of this phrase is that you make the various stratagems inside the camp curtains, and defeat your opponent while he is still a thousand miles away. This being so, there is an essential meaning for application of this verse to the martial arts, and that is to understand the interior of the camp curtains to be your mind.

You should understand "devising stratagems within the closed camp curtains" as having a mind free of negligence, watching the movements and activities of your opponents, devising various stratagems,[12] and watching your opponent for an opening. You should understand "victory is determined a thousand miles away" as watching your opponent for an opening and defeating him with the sword.

Leading a large army and being victorious in battle should be no different from performing the martial art of a match with swords. You should be victorious in a battle of great armies with an understanding of how to win by cutting someone down in a match with opposing swords; and you should be victorious in the martial art of a sword match with an understanding of battles with great armies.

Victory and defeat at the point of a sword are in the mind. Your hands and feet are also moved by the mind.

Concerning *jo* (preface), *ha* (breach), and *kyu* (dispatch),[13] there are combinations of three and nine, and thus twenty-seven cutting techniques:

> *Jo*: *Jodan* (3) *Chudan* (3) *Gedan*[14] (3)
> *Ha*: *Jodan* (3) *Chudan* (3) *Gedan* (3) *Tobo* *Kiriai* *Sekko*
> *Kyu*: *Jodan* (3) *Chudan* (3) *Gedan* (3)

All three are performed with a single beat.[15]

This chapter should be taught and learned by the teacher and student through sparring; it is not enough just to detail it in writing. For those who have made an exhaustive study of what is catalogued above, copy this chapter and present it to them. This will be proof that they are disciples of this school.

I inscribe this for the sake of my descendants.

> *Kamiizumi Musashi no kami Fujiwara Hidetsuna*
> *My late father, Yagyu Tajima no kami Taira Muneyoshi*
> *His son, Yagyu Tajima no kami Taira Munenori*

I have called this chapter the Shoe-Presenting Bridge because long ago Chang Liang presented the shoe to Shih-kung.[16] After the Way of the Martial Arts had been bequeathed to Chang Liang, Kao-tsu gained control of the empire by means of Chang Liang's stratagems,[17] and the Han dynasty was maintained for four hundred years. Thus, I have grasped the heart of this story and named this chapter the Shoe-Presenting Bridge.

You should make this chapter a bridge and cross it to the Way of the Martial Arts.

THE DEATH-DEALING SWORD

In ancient times it was said,

> Weapons are instruments of ill omen. The Way of Heaven finds them repugnant. The Way of Heaven is to use them only when necessary.[1]

If you would ask why this is so, it can be said that bows and arrows, swords, and halberds are called weapons, and further that these are instruments of bad fortune and ill omen. The reason for this is that the Way of Heaven is a Way that brings life,[2] while instruments that kill are, on the contrary, truly ill-omened. Thus they are considered repugnant because they are contrary to the Way of Heaven.

Nevertheless, it goes on to say that using weapons and killing people when this cannot be avoided is also the Way of Heaven. If you would ask what this means, it is that flowers bloom and greenery accompanies them in the spring breezes, but the leaves fall and trees wither when autumn frosts arrive. This is the judgment of the Way of Heaven.

There is reason in striking down something that is replete. A man may ride his good fortune and commit evil, but you strike him down when that evil is replete. Thus, it may be said that using weapons is also the Way of Heaven. There are times when ten thousand people suffer because of the evil of one man. Therefore, in killing one man's evil you give ten thousand people life. In such ways, truly, the sword that kills one man will be the blade that gives others life.

There is an art[3] to using those weapons. If you do not know this art, you may well be killed by the person whom you are trying to kill.

Think about this carefully. In what we are terming the martial arts, you stand off against another individual, both of you using a sword. In this martial art there will be only one person who wins and one person who loses. This is a very small martial art.[4] Although there is a victory and a defeat, the gain and loss will not be much. It is a large martial art when one person wins and the empire wins, or when one person loses and the empire loses. In this case, the "one person" is the general, and the "empire" is the various armed forces. The various armed forces are the hands and feet of the general. Making the various forces function well is making the general's hands and feet function well. When the various forces do not function well, the general's hands and feet do not function well.

In a match with two opposing swords, victory comes to the man who naturally harmonizes Principle and Function,[5] and whose hands and feet work well. In the same way it can be said that the martial art of the great general is in winning a battle by using his various forces well and by skillfully devising stratagems.

It goes without saying that when two opposing armies face one another and victory or defeat is to be determined on the battlefield, a general opposes those two armies in the few square inches of his mind and observes how he will lead his army into battle. This is a martial art performed in the mind.

It is a martial art to be mindful of chaotic times while ruling the country in peace; and it is also a martial art to observe the inner workings of a country, to know what causes chaos, and to rule well before chaos begins.

While you are governing a country, it is yet again a martial art to keep your mind clearly on the farthest corners of the farthest province and to appoint various officials to keep guard over them. Such officials—from the highest to lowest—may have their own selfish agendas, and the suffering of those under them could indeed be the beginning of the country's ruin.

Thus, it is essential that you observe the inner workings of the country and prevent its ruin at the hands of officials with various personal agendas. This is like the martial art of seeing into the intentions of your opponent in a sword match by observing his movements.[6]

You must observe the situation clearly and with great intensity! This is the Great Principle of the martial arts.

Again, a lord may be accompanied by flatterers who, when facing their superior, will put on the appearance of men of the Way; but when regarding their inferiors, will flash looks of anger. If one does not curry favor with such men, good deeds will be reported as evil, the guiltless will suffer and criminals will be praised. Observing this principle is more important than seeing through your opponent's intentions by the movements of his sword.

The province is the lord's province, and the people are the lord's people. Those close to the lord serving as administrators are his vassals, just as are those who serve him from afar. What matters the degree of intimacy? They are like hands and feet for the sake of the ruler. Are the feet different from the hands because they are farther away? If both are equal in concern, will one be more intimate and the other more remote?

Nevertheless, a man close to the lord may plunder those far away, and if the innocent are made to suffer, will they not resent even a lord who is without stain? Those close to the lord are few—no more than five or ten—but those at a distance are many. Now the many may resent the lord and sever their affections toward him, and the few close to the lord may have had their own interests in mind from the beginning. With no thought of true service, those few may govern in such a way as to make the people resent the lord, and at such a time will fight to be the first to distance themselves from him.

It is best to observe this principle well, so that those at a distance will not somehow be at a disadvantage, beyond their lord's blessings. If you observe this principle well, it will become your martial art.

Having no conflicts in association with friends from beginning to end is also a matter of seeing into the principles of a relationship, and this, too, is a martial art of the mind. The mind that looks into the principles of associating with people in a particular setting is a martial art as well. If you do not observe these principles you may overstay yourself at a certain gathering and incur shame for yourself for no real account. Or, by prattling on without observing the sensibilities of the people with whom you are associating, you may invite an argument or even bring yourself to ruin. All of this depends upon either seeing or not seeing into principles.

Arranging objects in your living room is a matter of using what is right for each place, and this, too, is a matter of seeing into the principles of those places. This is not unlike the very heart of the martial arts. Truly, the arena may change, but the principle is the same, and thus you could even apply this to national affairs and make no mistakes.

It is missing the point to think that the martial art is solely in cutting a man down. It is not in cutting people down; it is in killing evil. It is the stratagem of killing the evil of one man and giving life to ten thousand.

What is written down in these three chapters should not

leave this school, but this is not making a secret of the Way. To keep this in secret is for the sake of making it known.[7] Not making it known would be the same as not writing it down. You, my descendants, should think this over well.

The Great Learning[8] is the gate for the beginning scholar. For the most part, when arriving at a house you first go in through the gate. The gate is a sign that you have approached the house. Passing through this gate, you enter the house and meet the master. Just so, Learning is the gate that approaches the Way. Passing through *this* gate, you arrive at the Way. But Learning is the gate, not the house. Do not look at the gate and think, "This is the house." The house is within, reached only after passing through the gate.

Do not read written works and think, "This is the Way." Written works are like the gate to approach the Way. Thus, there are people who remain ignorant of the Way regardless of how much they have learned and how many Chinese characters they know. Though they face the pages and read as skillfully as though they were annotating the ancients, they are ignorant of the truth and so do not make the Way their own. Nevertheless, it is quite difficult to approach the Way without studying. Still, one cannot say that a man embodies the Way simply because he has studied and speaks well. There are also people who are naturally in harmony with the Way and who have never studied at all.

In *The Great Learning* it says, "Extend your knowledge to all things." [9] To "extend" means to do so exhaustively. Exhaustively extending your knowledge generally means to know men as they are in the world and to exhaustively know the principles of all existing things. To "extend your knowledge," then, is to have nothing said to be unknown. "All things" can also be read as "exhausting all things and events." If you exhaustively know the principles of all things, there is nothing remaining unknown, and nothing that cannot be done.

When you have left no stone unturned in knowledge, you have done the same with all things. But if you do not know the principles, nothing will come of your actions.

If you do not know all things, you still harbor doubts. And when you doubt something, that thing will not leave your mind. If you come to the end of a matter with the principle clearly understood, there will be nothing at all in your mind. This is called exhausting knowledge and exhausting the things of this world.

When there is nothing at all left in your mind, everything becomes easy to do. The study of all Ways is done for the sake of making a clean sweep of your mind. Because in the beginning a man knows nothing at all, he has nothing at all in his mind. [10]

When you begin to study, there is something in your mind; you are obstructed by that thing, and it becomes difficult to do anything at all. If you can clear from your mind those things you have learned, they too will become nothing; and when you perform the techniques of the various Ways, the techniques will come easily regardless of what you have learned and without being contrary to it. When you perform an action you will be in harmony with what you have learned, without even being aware of it.

You should understand that this is the Way of the martial arts. The heart of "extending knowledge" is the discipline of exhaustively learning a hundred methods with the sword and thoroughly mastering the postures, methods of using the eyes, and the other techniques.

When you have run the length of various practices and none of those practices remain in your mind, that very lack of mind itself is the heart of "all things." When you have exhaustively learned the various practices and techniques and made great efforts in disciplined training, there will be action in your arms, legs, and body but none in your mind; you will have distanced yourself from training, but will not be in opposition to it, and you will have freedom in whatever techniques you perform. You yourself will be unaware of where your mind is, and neither demons nor heresies will be able to find it. Training is done for the purpose of reaching this state. With successful training, training falls away. This is the secret principle toward which all Ways progress.

By forgetting about training and casting off your mind, you will be all the more unaware of yourself. The place you come to in this way is the perfection of the Way. At this level, you enter through training and arrive at its very absence.

CH'I AND WILL

The mind that takes up its stance within and intently considers a matter is called the will. The will is internal, but when it is manifested externally it is called *ch'i*.[11] The will can be said to be the master, and *ch'i* the servant. Will is internal and uses *ch'i*. If *ch'i* overruns its bounds, it stumbles. *Ch'i* is reined in by will, and should not be made to hurry.

In terms of the martial arts, we call will the concentration of the mind from the waist down, and *ch'i* the giving and receiving of strikes when a match is in progress. The mind should be thoroughly concentrated below the waist and the *ch'i* should not be driven too precipitously. It is essential to remain calm, so that *ch'i* is reined in by will, and will is not dragged along by *ch'i*.

Deception is the foundation of the martial arts[12]

Deception is strategy. By the false, the truth is obtained.[13] Deception is such that, even when your opponent is aware of it, he cannot help but be taken in. When you use deception and your opponent is taken in, you defeat him by causing him to be taken in. When you see that your opponent has not been taken in, you use yet another deception. Thus even an opponent not initially taken in can be taken in after all.

In Buddhism this is called an "expedient means."[14] The truth is hidden within, a ruse is placed without, and in the end one is drawn onto the Path of Truth. In this way, all deception becomes truth. In the Shinto religion, this is called "mystery." By the mysterious, men's faith is aroused; and when there is faith there will be divine favor.

In the warrior clans this is called military strategy. Though strategy is deception, it is through deception that victory is obtained without hurting others. This way, deception becomes truth in the end. This is called "putting things in order by applying the contrary."

In Zen there is a saying, "Beat the grass and scare up the snake." Just as you beat the grass to scare up the snake that lies within, there is a technique of surprising your opponent to cause his mind to become agitated. Deception is doing something unexpected by your opponent, and surprising him. This is the martial arts.

Once surprised, your opponent's mind will be taken, and his skill undone. Raising your fan or hand in front of him will also take your opponent's mind. Tossing aside the sword you are carrying is also a martial art. If you have attained the skill of No-Sword,[15] what will a sword be to you? Another man's sword is your sword. This is the function of "Grasping the Opportunity."[16]

The heart of Grasping the Opportunity (*kizen*) is always in grasping the moving power from your opponent. The character *ki* refers to the *ch'i* concentrated within one's mind. This *ki* is *ch'i*. Observing your opponent's *ch'i* and moving to meet the opponent before his *ch'i* can function is Grasping the Opportunity. This action also exists in Zen, as is clear from the phrase, "the moving power of Zen."[17]

Ki is the unmanifested *ch'i* hidden within. As a controlling power it can be likened to the hidden device in a door that allows it to be opened and shut. Acting by an astute observation of this almost unseen[18] and unmanifested *ch'i* hidden inside is known in the martial arts as Grasping the Opportunity.

On the words *ken* (Attacking) and *tai* (Abiding)

Attacking means assaulting intensely: striking the first blow[19] with your sword with all your concentration as soon as you meet your opponent. This attitude is the same, whether it is within your opponent's mind or your own.

Abiding means waiting for your opponent to make the first move, and not making an abrupt attack yourself. You should understand Abiding to mean exercising extreme caution.

Attacking and Abiding: these two mean assaulting and waiting.

The principles of Attacking and Abiding exist in both the body and the sword.

Attack your opponent by closely approaching him with your body and yet holding back with your sword. In this way, you entice him to make the first move with your body and limbs, and defeat him by that enticement. So doing, your body and limbs are Attacking while your sword is Abiding. Putting the body and limbs in Attack is done to cause your opponent to make the first move.

Attacking and Abiding exist in both body and mind

You should hold the mind in a state of Abiding and the body in Attack. This is because if the mind is in Attack, it will run to excess until the effect is a negative one. Restrain your mind and carry it in Abiding; have your body Attack and defeat your opponent by making him take the first step. If your mind takes the attitude of Attack, you will feel that you must cut your opponent first, and you will suffer defeat.

On the other hand, there is also an understanding of having the mind in Attack and the body in Abiding. The heart of this is in working your mind without negligence. By having your mind in Attack and your sword in Abiding, you cause your opponent to take the first step. In this case, you should understand "the body" to be nothing other than the hand holding your sword. Thus we say that the mind is in Attack and the body in Abiding.

Although these two definitions exist, they ultimately mean the same. Either way, you obtain the victory by having your opponent make the first move.

Lessons on how to approach an opponent when he takes up Attack

- Two Stars[20]
- Peak and Valley[21]
- Distant Plaited Mountains[22]

All these items are ways of observing, or fixing the eyes. The details are transmitted orally.

- The Rhythm of Far and Near[23]
- Body Position and Sensation of the Bead Tree[24]

These two items are concerned with the sword and body posture.

- Making a shield of your fists
- Placing the body sideways
- Keeping your shoulders level with your opponent's fists
- Keeping your rear leg open
- Keeping your stance the same as your opponent's

These five items are concerned with both the body and the sword. Each should be learned while you are engaged in matches. They are difficult to express in written words.

Well then, the mentality for each of these five items is to fully concentrate your mind below the waist, to be completely attentive, and to have no negligence in your mind before engaging with your opponent. While engaged, your mind should be unwobbling. These things are essential.

If you lack the concentration below the waist and suddenly have to fight, neither the techniques you have learned nor anything else will come to your aid.

Lessons on how to approach an opponent when he takes an attitude of Abiding

- Two Stars
- Peaks and Valleys
- Distant Mountains

When your opponent has taken a strict attitude of Abiding, these three targets for fixing the eyes should not be abandoned. Simply, these targets for fixing the eyes should be used for both Attack and Abiding; they are essential. You should bear clearly in mind that Peaks is for striking attacks and that Distant Mountains is for exchanging strikes and close-in fighting. Generally, you should always fix your eyes on the Two Stars.

The Three Intents

The Three Intents are nothing other than three observations. They consist of a trial attack of striking, drawing, and waiting.[25] When it is difficult to gauge what your opponent is going to do, you should be able to discern his intentions with these. They are used to sound out the mind of your opponent. For an opponent who has resolutely set himself into an attitude of Abiding, use these three or similar provocations, execute your deception, make your opponent use his own technique, and defeat him.

Adhere to a Change, Follow a Change[26]

The heart of this matter is that if your opponent has taken an attitude of Abiding and you provoke him with a number of changes, your opponent himself will then manifest change.[27] Following that change, you will defeat him.

Manipulating Two Eyes[28]

You should execute various deceptions with an opponent who has taken an attitude of Abiding. While watching what your opponent is doing, you should look when you do not seem to be doing so, and not look when you seem to be looking. Do not be negligent at any moment, and do not set your eyes on any one place but keep them moving steadily and quickly.

In a certain Chinese poem, it is said,

> With a pilfered glance,[29] the dragonfly evades the shrike.

A "pilfered glance" means a stealthy look. In order to avoid being caught, the dragonfly looks stealthily in the direction of the shrike and leaps into flight. You should constantly, without negligence, look stealthily at your opponent's actions.

The mind that defeats the opponent by allowing him to strike

To cut a man with a single blow is easy. To avoid being cut by a man is difficult. Though a man intends to strike you and advances to do so, keep him at a certain interval, above all remain calm and allow him to advance, and then allow him to strike. Thus, even though your opponent has an intention to strike and goes through the motions of striking, if you maintain a certain interval, he will not make contact. The sword that makes no contact is a dead sword. You then go over his dead sword, strike, and defeat him.

Your opponent's first strike has missed, but in return, you take him with the first strike of your sword.

After you have struck your first blow, be sure to prevent him from lifting his hands again. After you strike, if you vacillate about what to do next, your opponent will surely strike at you with yet another blow. At this point, negligence will equal defeat. You will be struck by your opponent and your first strike will be brought to nothing. This is because your mind stopped at the point you placed your blow. Do not rest your mind at the place you have struck, wondering whether you have cut the man or not. You should strike him a second or third time, and yet a fourth or fifth time, not giving him a chance to even raise his face.

The victory will be determined by the first blow of your sword.

THREE RHYTHMS[30]

One rhythm is when you and your opponent strike at the same time; another is when he raises his sword and you strike from beneath; and a third is when he lowers his sword and you go over it and strike.

The rhythm of striking at the same time is considered to be

undesirable,[31] while a rhythm of striking separately is thought to be good. If the strikes are simultaneous, your opponent will be able to use his sword well; but if the strikes are not made at the same moment, he will use his sword poorly. You should strike so that it is difficult for your opponent to use his sword. Whether you attack from below or above, you should strike with No-Beat.[32]

Generally speaking, it is undesirable to maintain a rhythm.

Broad[33] Rhythm, Short[34] Rhythm; Short Rhythm, Broad Rhythm

If your opponent brandishes his sword and establishes a broad rhythm, you should brandish your sword with a short rhythm. If your opponent establishes a short rhythm, you should use a broad rhythm. This, too, is understood as using a rhythm to keep your opponent out of rhythm. If you maintain a rhythm, your opponent will be able to use his sword well.

A skillful chanter of Noh drama, for example, will perform in such a way as to maintain no particular rhythm, and an unskilled drummer will be unable to play along with him. In the same way that chanting or drumming will be difficult if there is a skillful chanter but a poor drummer, or a skillful drummer but a poor chanter, the combinations of broad-and-short rhythm or short-and-broad rhythm will make it difficult for your opponent to strike.

If an unskillful chanter falls into a broad rhythm, an accomplished drummer may try to beat lightly with a short rhythm but will be unsuccessful. Again, if a skillful chanter takes up a light beat, a poor drummer will be unable to keep from falling behind.

A skillful birdcatcher will first let the bird see his pole, then shake the pole loosely from his end and, with a smooth approach, capture the bird. The bird is taken in by the shaking rhythm of the pole. Though it flutters its wings again and again, it is unable to take flight and so is caught.

You should act so that you are out of rhythm with your opponent. If the rhythm is upset, he will not even be able to jump over a ditch, but will step right into it. You should give careful scrutiny to this kind of mentality.

BEING AWARE OF THE ENTIRE SONG

For both dance and chanting, you will be unable to perform if you do not know the entire song. You should understand the Entire Song in the martial arts as well. You should especially see through your opponent and ascertain the action of his sword. Know this through to the bottom of his mind and you will have the mind that has memorized the Entire Song well.

If you know the demeanor and action of your opponent well, you will gain freedom in your own devices.

- Counterstriking[35]
- Two or Three Inches Between Combatants[36]
- Quickly Stealing the Body[37]

- Checking the *Jodan* Interlace[38]
- Checking the Space Between Right and Left During a Wheel Sword Maneuver[39]
- The Three-Foot Interval[40]

These six items will not be learned unless transmitted orally and taught during matches with the master. They are not to be expressed by putting everything down with brush and paper.

There may be occasions when you brandish your sword using various feints and deceptions with techniques such as these, and your opponent, taking a firm attitude of Abiding, will neither be startled nor made to initiate a move. When this occurs, steal within three feet of your opponent and draw up close to his body. When he can bear this no longer, allow him to move to make his first strike, and then strike. If your opponent does not strike, it is likely that you will be unable to defeat him. If your opponent *does* strike at you, keep the no-contact interval clearly in mind, and he will not be able to strike abruptly at you again.

Practice this technique well, move close to your opponent without timidity, get him to make the first move, and defeat him. This is the concept of Initiating the Initial Move.[41]

- The Great Distortion[42] and the Feint Attack. This should be orally transmitted.
- Mindfulness:[43] To be maintained in both Attacking and Abiding. This should be orally transmitted.

- Avoiding the Opponent's Sword by Keeping Open a Foot and a Half.[44]
- Engaging Attack and Abiding: You should understand the body in Attack and the sword in Abiding.

All of these items will be difficult to master if they are not transmitted orally and learned during matches with the master.

LISTENING TO THE SOUND OF WIND AND WATER[45]

The foundation of this Way is always deception.[46] Its wisdom of victory is entirely in attacking with various feints, creating variations, and causing the opponent to make the first move. Even *before* the fight, you must be resolved that your opponent will attack,[47] and not be negligent. It is essential to maintain your concentration below the waist.

If you do not think your opponent will attack, you will be set upon quickly and severely as soon as the fight begins, and all your daily training and techniques will be for naught. After the attack begins, it is essential to put your mind, body, and legs in Attack, and your hands[48] in an attitude of Abiding. You must look and pay careful attention to Existence.[49] This is the lesson of Grasping Existence. Indeed, if you do not observe this aspect with calm, it is unlikely that your lessons in swordsmanship will be of much use.

Listening to Wind and Water means tranquillity above and intense activity below. The voice of the wind does not exist, but issues forth when it comes in contact with things. Thus, when it blows high above, it is tranquil; but when it blows below and touches trees, bamboo and the myriad things, its voice is hurried and loud. Water, too, when falling from above, has no voice; but when it comes in contact with things and falls on what is below, there will be a clattering sound.

Tranquillity is above and intense activity is below. This is to say, the exterior is calm and peaceful, with nothing to invite a second look, while the interior is attentive and free of negligence.

It is undesirable to have the body and the limbs hurry. Attacking and Abiding[50] should be placed within and without. It is not right to harden into just one of these two. Remember that Yin and Yang go through their changes mutually. Movement is Yang; tranquillity is Yin. Yin and Yang move—now inside, now out. When Yang moves within, the outside is tranquil with Yin. If Yin is within, Yang moves and is manifested outside. The martial arts are like this as well: moving without negligence, activating the *ch'i* within, and keeping the outside peaceful, with no cause for alarm.

It is in accord with the principle of Heaven that Yang moves within, and that Yin is peaceful without. Moreover, if Attack moves rigorously on the outside, the mind within should remain calm and unaffected by the exterior. In this way, even though the exterior is in Attack, it will not be in disorder.

If both interior and exterior are in motion, there will be disorder. You should make Attacking and Abiding, motion and tranquillity, and interior and exterior all mutual.

The waterbird floats along the surface of the water and, though tranquil above, paddles along on webbed feet below. In the same way, if you are without negligence within and make great efforts with this practice, mind and body will unify, inside and outside will become one, and you will be without hindrance. Reaching this sphere, you will have obtained the very ultimate.

SICKNESS

To think only of winning is sickness. To think only of using the martial arts is sickness. To think only of demonstrating the result of one's training is sickness, as is thinking only of making an attack or waiting for one. To think in a fixated way only of expelling such sickness is also sickness. Whatever remains absolutely in the mind should be considered sickness. As these various sicknesses are all present in the mind, you must put your mind in order and expel them.

An Understanding of the Two Levels[51] for Expelling Sickness:[52] The Preliminary Level

"Use thought to arrive at No-Thought; use attachment to be nonattached."[53] The heart of this is that thinking of expelling sickness is itself a thought. The thought of expelling sickness in the mind is "using a thought."[54] It is also called sickness when you are consumed by a thought.

To think of expelling sickness is a thought. However, you may expel thought by the use of thought. When you can leave off thoughts, you will have become void of them.[55] In this way, using thoughts is said to be No-Thought. If you can expel the sickness of any remaining thoughts with thought, afterward both the thought that has been expelled and the thought with which it was expelled will disappear. This is the same as using a wedge to extract another wedge. If you drive a wedge into the place where another wedge is stuck, the first wedge will loosen and come out. When the first wedge is extracted, the wedge used to loosen it will not remain either.

If you wish to expel sickness, the thought that is used to expel sickness will not remain afterward, and this is called "using thought to arrive at No-Thought." The thought of expelling sickness may be an attachment to that sickness, but with that attachment sickness is expelled, and the attachment itself does not remain. This is called "Using an attachment to become nonattached."

The Profound Level

In the profound level, expelling sickness is in the lack of mind that thinks only of doing so. The thought of expelling sickness is itself sickness. Sickness will be expelled by abandoning yourself to it, and carrying on within its midst.

The thought of expelling sickness will not have results because that thought is in the mind. Thus, the more the sickness remains and the more you become fixated on that thought, the less benefit there will be. How should this be understood?

The answer is this:[56] the preliminary and the profound have been established in two levels for this use. When you train yourself in the preliminary frame of mind and have acquired [sufficient] discipline, the fixation is left behind without even the thought of leaving it.

What is called "sickness" is fixation. In Buddhism, fixation is abhorred. The monk who has left fixation behind, however, can mingle with the dust of worldly affairs and not be stained; he is free in whatever he does, and abides in no one place. Experts in all the Ways can hardly be called masters if, beyond their various techniques, they have not yet severed themselves from fixation.[57]

Dust and dirt will become attached to a rough, unpolished gem. The polished gem, however, will be unblemished even in the midst of the mire. By means of discipline, you polish the jewel of the mind, allowing no blemish; you abandon yourself to sickness, and toss away the mind altogether.

A monk asked an ancient worthy, "What is the Way?" The worthy replied, "Your ordinary mind, that is the Way."[58]

This anecdote contains a principle that runs through all disciplines. When an explanation of the Way is requested, the answer is "your ordinary mind." This is truly profound. Expelling all the sicknesses of the mind, engendering the *ordinary* mind, and yet abiding amidst sickness . . . this is the state of being without sickness.

Apply this to the world of the arts. When practicing archery, if your mind is occupied by thoughts of shooting the bow, your aim will be disordered and wandering. When using the sword, if your mind is occupied with thoughts of plying the sword, its tip will not likely be regulated. When practicing calligraphy, if your mind is occupied by thoughts of writing, the brush will be unsettled. When playing the *koto*, if your mind is filled with thoughts of plucking the strings, the melody will be confused.

When the man shooting the bow forgets about the mind that is shooting the bow and releases the string with the ordinary mind he has when doing nothing, the bow will be tranquil. When plying a sword, riding a horse, writing something, or playing the *koto*, take up the ordinary mind that does none of these or anything at all. Then no matter what you do, you will do it with ease.

No matter which discipline you follow, if you have in your breast one absolute course, it will not be the real Way. The man who has nothing at all in his breast is a real "Man of the Way." Having nothing in his breast, when he does something it is done with ease, no matter what arises.

Because a mirror is always clear and has no form within it at all, the form of whatever stands before it will be clearly reflected. The breast of a Man of the Way is like a mirror: it does nothing and is perfectly clear. Thus, he has No-Mind, and in all things lacks nothing. This is the ordinary mind. A man who accomplishes everything with this ordinary mind is said to be a master.

In doing any number of things, you hold the mind that does it correctly,[59] and do not scatter that mind distractedly. But in doing that one thing with a single purpose, you will do it inconsistently. Just when you think you've done something well once, you do it again, but poorly. Or, if you do something well twice and do it poorly the third time, you may congratulate yourself for doing well two out of three times; but then once again you do poorly and nothing is settled. This is because you do it with a mind occupied with doing something well.

When you have continuously made great efforts and have accumulated discipline without really noticing, you will have left aside the thought of doing things well, and will have attained the realm of No-Mind/No-Thought. And this, without really thinking about it and no matter what you do. Your actions will be like the machinations of a wooden puppet. At such a time, you will not be self-conscious and your mind will not be occupied with what you are doing. Thus, in ten out of ten times, your body, hands, and feet will make no mistakes. But if your mind slips in even slightly, you will miss your aim. When you have No-Mind, you will hit the mark every time.

No-Mind, however, is not a state of having no mind at all. It is simply your ordinary mind.

Like a Man Made of Wood, with Flowers and Birds

These are the words of Layman P'ang.[60] They refer to being like a man made of wood facing flowers and birds. Though flowers and birds are right before its eyes, its heart is not moved. This is reasonable, as a man made of wood has no heart. So how can you, a man having a heart, be like one made of wood?

The man of wood is a metaphor. As a human being with a heart, you should not be equivalent to wood. As a human being, you should not be like wood or bamboo at all.

This is not a matter of looking at flowers and newly engendering a mind that is engaged in this activity. What is said here is that one looks with the ordinary mind, with No-Mind.[61] Shooting a bow is not a matter of doing so while newly preparing the mind for such an activity. What is said here is that you shoot with the ordinary mind.

The ordinary mind is said to be No-Mind. If you change the ordinary mind and engender it anew, insofar as the form will be modified, both interior and exterior will move. If you do everything with a wobbling mind, nothing will be as it should. If a man speaks in an unwobbling manner, though it be a single word, he will be praised.[62] The Unmoving Mind of all the Buddhas is truly felt to be admirable.

"The Profound Level" and this section are helpful in possessing a mind that can expel the sickness of the martial arts.

The priest Chung-feng[63] said, "Maintain the mind that releases the mind."

This saying has two levels of meaning.

The practice of the first is as follows: if you "release" the mind, do not allow it to become fixated when it reaches its destination, but unfailingly make it return. If you strike once with your sword, do not let your mind stop at that strike, but bring your mind back securely to yourself.[64]

The deeper meaning is: in releasing the mind, you let it go where it wishes.[65] "Releasing the mind" means letting it go and not letting it stop anywhere. "Maintain the mind that releases the mind" means exactly that, for if the mind is released and always brought back as if in a net, it will not be free. The mind that releases the mind is one that is let go and does not stop. If you maintain such a released mind, your movements will be free.

Even dogs and cats are better raised unleashed. A leashed dog or a leashed cat cannot be raised well.

Those who read the Confucian scriptures become fixated on the word "reverence."[66] When they place this concept above all others and live their whole lives by it alone, they make their minds resemble a leashed cat.

We also have the word "reverence" in Buddhism, and the sutras speak of the "Undisturbed Concentrated Mind."[67] These two would seem to be very close in meaning. You concentrate your mind on one thing, and allow no confusion from any direction. Of course there is also the chanted phrase, "Speaking with reverence is itself the Buddha and all his disciples." And when facing a Buddhist image, one is said to "concentrate on a respectful salutation." None of these differ with the intent of the word "reverence."

Nevertheless, all of these are expedients for pacifying the

disturbed mind, and the mind that is well pacified will not need an expedient.

When you intone the name of Lord Fudo[68] you make your posture correct, press your palms together, and contemplate his unmoving form in your consciousness. At this time, the Three Conditions of Karma—body, mouth, and consciousness[69]—are made one and equal, and concentration is undisturbed. This is called the Universalization of the Three Mysteries.[70]

In intent, therefore, these are the same as the word "reverence"; and "reverence" is in harmony with the virtue of the Original Mind.

This condition of the mind, however, lasts only while you are performing the ritual. If you release your palms and stop intoning the Buddha's Name,[71] the Buddhist image in your mind disappears, and you return once again to your confused mental state. This is not a totally pacified mind.[72]

The man who has been able to pacify his mind once and for all from beginning to end may not have cleansed the Three Conditions of body, mouth, and consciousness, but he can mingle with the dust of the world and remain unstained. Though he moves through the world all day long, he himself is unmovable. This is like the moon that seems to follow the innumerable waves, yet truly moves not at all. This is the sphere of one who has reached the ultimate of the Buddhist Law.

I write this down as the instructions I received from a Buddhist priest.[73]

THE LIFE-GIVING SWORD[1]

A HUNDRED STANCES

Although there are a hundred kinds of stances, they all exist for the same purpose: to defeat the opponent.

The above, at its extreme, is the *shuji shuriken*.[2]

Though you may teach or learn a hundred postures or myriad techniques, the *shuji shuriken* alone is considered to be the eye of one's actions. Though both you and your opponent may know a hundred different stances, the match itself will be brought to an end by using the *shuji shuriken*. Because this is a secret tradition, we do not write the word down with its true Chinese characters, but write characters that sound the same.

The Rhythm of Existence and Non-Existence.[3]

This is the lesson of Existence and Non-Existence in relation to *shuji shuriken*. When manifested, it is existence; when hidden, it is non-existence. The hidden and manifested existence and non-existence are exactly *shuji shuriken.*

It is in the hand that grasps the sword.

In Buddhism, there is also this matter of existence and non-existence, and we can speak of that as a model.

The common run of man sees existence but does not see non-existence. With *shuji shuriken* you see both existence and non-existence; existence exists and non-existence exists. At a moment of existence, you strike at existence; at a moment of non-existence, you strike at non-existence. Also, without waiting for existence, you strike at non-existence, and without waiting for non-existence, you strike at existence. To this extent, it is said that existence is existence, and non-existence is also existence.

In the scripture of Lao Tzu[4] it is said,

> In the Unchanging, there is Existence;
> In the Unchanging, there is Non-Existence.[5]

So existence is always present, as is non-existence. When hidden, existence is non-existence; when manifested, non-existence is existence.

For example, when a waterbird floats on the water, it is existence; when it goes under the water, it is non-existence. Thus, even when you think, "This is existence," know that it is also non-existence when it is hidden. And again, when you think, "This is non-existence," know that it is existence when manifested.

In this way, the concepts of existence and non-existence are only consequential on being hidden or manifested. Their existence is one. Thus, both existence and non-existence are always within the Unchanging.

In Buddhism, these are called Fundamental Non-Existence and Fundamental Existence. At a person's death, the existent is hidden; when a person is born, the non-existent is manifested. The essence of these two is in the Unchanging.

We say that existence and non-existence are in the hand that grasps the sword, and this is a secret tradition. It is called the *shuji shuriken*. When the hand lies flat, existence is hidden; when the palm faces upward, non-existence is manifested. We can say this, but if the teaching is not transmitted directly from person to person, the words are difficult to understand.

When there is existence, you should see it and strike it. When there is non-existence, you should see that and strike it.

Thus it is said that both existence and non-existence are existence. That which is called existence is nothing other than non-existence, and that which is called non-existence is none other than existence. Existence and non-existence are not two; if you see the existence and non-existence of *shuji shuriken* as different, you will not likely be victorious, though you may work exhaustively through a hundred techniques. The myriad styles of the martial arts are ultimately to be found in this one step.

THE MOON ON WATER AND ITS REFLECTION[6]

The phrase "moon on water" refers to the fact that if there is a certain distance between you and your opponent, his sword will be unable to strike you. In keeping this distance, we use the martial arts. Stepping inside this distance and stealing close to your opponent without his noticing is like piercing the reflection of the moon on water.

You should establish this Moon on Water in your mind before the start of the match, and then meet your opponent. The distance itself should be orally transmitted.

THE MYSTERIOUS SWORD AND MINDFULNESS OF THE SEAT KEPT IN BODY AND LEGS

The "Mysterious Sword" is of ultimate importance and indicates a place on the body.[7] When referring to yourself, the character for "sword" of the Mysterious Sword should be written just as it is, and understood as "sword." Whether in a stance to the right or left, your own sword does not leave the seat of the Mysterious Sword. The heart of this phrase is in the Chinese character for "sword."

When referring to your opponent, the word "sword" should be written and understood as the word "to observe."[8] You clearly observe the seat of your opponent's Mysterious Sword and then cut deeply into him, so this point of observation is essential. Thus the understanding of the word as "observation."

The Two Chinese Characters, *Shin* and *Myo*[9]

Shin resides within, while *myo* is manifest without. Thus the word *shinmyo*, or the Mysterious.

Let me explain the meaning of the two words *shin* and *myo*. *Shin* exists within, and *myo* is manifested without. This is called *shinmyo*, or the Mysterious. For example, because *shin* resides within a tree, flowers bloom and are fragrant, the color green appears, and the branches and leaves grow thick. These are called *myo*. Break the tree into fragments and you will be unable to see this *shin*, but without it there will not likely be flowers and leaves on the outside.

For the human being as well, though you split open his body, you will be unable to see anything you can identify as *shin*. Nevertheless, it is because *shin* lies within that one is able to perform various acts and deeds.

Because *shin* is placed in the seat of the Mysterious Sword, various *myo* are manifested in the hands and feet, and flowers are made to bloom in the midst of battle.

Shin acts as the master of the mind.[10] *Shin* is inside but uses the mind outside.[11] Further, the mind employs the use of *ch'i*. It uses *ch'i* and remains outside for the sake of *shin*. Now if this mind were to remain in one place, its uses would be for naught. This being so, it is essential for the mind not to stay in one place.

A master of men, for example, resides inside and sends his servant outside on an errand. If the servant stops at his destination and does not return home, his use is, likewise, for naught.

If your mind stops at something and does not return to its original quality, your skill in the martial arts will be truncated. For this reason it is not only in the martial arts that you do not stop the mind in one place. This principle extends to all things.

This understanding contains these two: *shin* and the mind.

- Expelling Sickness: Three Points[12] Sickness Within the Opponent
- Fixing the Eyes,[13] Holding a Rhythm (these should be transmitted orally)
- Stepping[14]

It is undesirable to be either fast or slow in taking steps. It is better to do so as you would ordinarily: smoothly and without self-consciousness. One takes the middle way, neither going too far nor failing to go far enough. Going fast is a result of consternation or fright; going slow is a result of fear and being overawed by the opponent. In any and all cases, you should never be thrown off balance.

If a man's eyes are open and you wave a folding fan in front of him, he will blink. Blinking in this case is the ordinary state of mind and is not a matter of being thrown off balance. But do this a number of times, flapping your fan two or three times to startle the man. If he doesn't blink at all, he has moved inwardly.

The mind resists being made to blink, thinking, " I'm *not* going to do this!" and it actually succeeds. Thus it moves actively from the bottom up. If an object comes at the eye in ordinary circumstances, the eye will blink unconsciously.

It is essential not to lose the mentality of this ordinary state of mind. If you think, "I won't move!" you have in fact already done so. Moving is itself the principle of not being moved. That a man blinks is the ordinary. In not blinking, the mind moves.

It is better to step smoothly in an ordinary way, without changing your ordinary mind. This is the realm of form and mind not being thrown off balance.

THE ONE PRINCIPLE[15]

This is the mental attitude when facing an opponent directly; also, the frame of mind when spears are used.

Generally speaking in the martial arts, whatever you do, you do freely. Thus, it is a very serious affair if you end up in a difficult situation. Being mindful of just this, paying close attention, and being careful not to fall into a sudden disaster—these together are called the One Principle.[16] The caution you use when facing an opponent directly at close range, or when facing an opponent with spears at a distance of five inches to a foot is also the One Principle. This is also the caution you use in difficult situations— for instance, when you cannot retreat because there is a wall or partition at your back and yet your opponent continues to advance toward you. The One Principle should be understood for situations of extreme gravity or difficulty.

It will be very difficult to act when you have no sword and misjudge the foot and a half, or when you stare at one particular place, become fixated on one action, or become negligent. Keeping such things in mind is called the One Principle, and is something to be kept secret.

You and Your Opponent—One Foot Each

This is the caution used when both swords are the same length, or when you do not have a sword.[17]

For you and your opponent alike, the implement of the sword will extend one foot from the body. At one foot, you can avoid his strike. It is dangerous to get any closer than one foot.

THE CORRECT AND ULTIMATE SINGLE STROKE

The Correct and Ultimate means the very ultimate. The Single Stroke is not in the sword. It is in observing the indications [of the intentions] of your opponent; this teaching is considered secret. The unsurpassed secret principle of this important Single Stroke is in watching your opponent's *actions*. You should understand this: the observation of your opponent's intentions is the First, or Single, Stroke; the blow of your sword according to your opponent's action is the second stroke.

Make this your foundation and you will be able to use it in a number of different ways. These are the *shuriken*, the Moon on Water, the Mysterious Sword, and Sickness. These four and one more, movement of the hands and feet, make five. We learn these as the Five Insights, One Observation.[18] Watching the *shuriken* is called the One Observation; the remaining four are held in the mind and are thus called Insights.

What you see with the eye is called observation; what you see with the mind is called an insight.[19] This is the significance of meditation, or seeing through your own thoughts.[20]

The fact that we don't say Four Insights, One Observation is because we group these all together and call them the Five Insights. Among them, we call *shuriken* the One Observation.

Shuriken, the Moon on Water, the Mysterious Sword, Sickness, and the Body and Limbs—these are the Five Insights. Among them, four are seen through the mind, but observing the *shuriken* with the eyes is called the One Observation.

Classification of the Moon on Water, the Mysterious Sword, Sickness, and the Body and Limbs

> The Moon on Water[21] is judging location[22] in a match
> The Mysterious Sword[23] is judging the location on the body
> The Body and Limbs
>> Observing your opponent's movements
>> Your own movements
> Sickness: for observing the *shuriken*

Thus, the ultimate point here is that it is essential to see what is manifested and what is not yet manifested in the *shuriken*. The four are really generalities. Expelling sickness is done in order to see the *shuriken*. If you cannot expel sickness, you will surely be taken by it, and your sight will be faulty. If your sight is faulty, you will lose. What is called sickness is a sickness of the mind, and a sickness of the mind is said to be the mind's stopping here and there.

You should act so as not to stop in the place you have struck with your sword. This is discarding, and yet not discarding the mind.

When your opponent takes a stance and confronts you with the tip of his sword, you should strike him as he raises his sword.[24]

If you want to strike your opponent, you should let him strike at you. If your opponent strikes at you, he himself will already have been struck.

Take the location of the Moon on Water. From that point, you should pay great attention to the way you maintain your mind and the way it acts. If you desire to take a certain location and your opponent has already taken it himself, you should parry the situation by considering it your choice. If your intentions do not change, the distance between you and your opponent will be the same, regardless of whether he was the one to establish it as five feet, or you were.

If a man has taken a certain place, it is best to let him do so and let it go. It is undesirable to become fixated on one certain place. Your body carriage should be light.

The placement of the feet and arrangement of the body

should be done so as not to become detached from the seat of the Mysterious Sword. You should be mindful of this and consider it before the match begins.

SEEING THE MYSTERIOUS SWORD: CLASSIFICATION OF THREE LEVELS[25]

It is considered fundamental to see with the mind. It is exactly because we see with the mind that the eyes also come into play. Thus, seeing with the eyes is second to seeing with the mind.

After seeing with the eyes, we should next see with the body and limbs. Acting so that your body and limbs do not become detached from your opponent's Mysterious Sword is called "seeing with the body and limbs."

Seeing with the mind is in order to see with the eyes. Seeing with the eyes is in order to apply the hands and feet to the seat of your opponent's Mysterious Sword.

> *The mind is like the moon on the water*
> *Form is like the reflection in a mirror.*

This verse suggests that the mentality proper for the martial arts is that of the moon's abiding in the water. It is also the reflection of your body abiding in the mirror. Man's mind moves to an object like the moon moves[26] to the water. How spontaneously this happens!

You should compare the seat of the Mysterious Sword to the

water and compare your mind to the moon, and move the mind to the seat of the Mysterious sword. When the mind moves, the body will move there as well. If the mind goes, the body will go. The body itself follows the mind.

This verse is used at the heart of this so that you may compare the mirror to the seat of the Mysterious Sword, and let your body move there just like a reflection. The significance of this is in not detaching your hands and feet from the seat of the Mysterious Sword.

The moon moves its reflection to the water with remarkable immediacy. Though it may be high up in the distant sky, its reflection pierces the water as soon as the clouds move aside. This is not something that comes down from the heavens gradually or by degrees and is then reflected. It is reflected faster than you can blink your eyes.

This, then, is a simile: man's mind moves to an object as quickly as the moon pierces the water.

In the Buddhist scriptures, it also likens the swiftness of the mind to the moon on water, or an image in a mirror. The meaning of this is *not* that the moon moves to the water, seems surely to be there, but disappears when you scoop it up from the bottom. The heart of this is simply that it is reflected immediately, just as it is, from the high heavens above.

As soon as something—no matter what—faces a mirror, its image enters that mirror immediately. This is a simile for alacrity.

Man's mind moves to an object just like this. His mind can

go to T'ang China in the blink of an eye. And just when you thought you might take a little nap, in a dream you may go off to your old hometown, more than a thousand miles away. The Buddha taught that the mind moves like this by using the similes of the moon on the water and an image in a mirror.

The poem above means the same when applied to the Moon on Water in the martial arts. Your mind should move like the moon. When the mind goes, the body goes as well. So after a match has begun, you should move your body to places just as a reflection moves in a mirror. If you have not kept your concentration below the waist, however, your body will not move. The Moon on Water is to each place as your body is to the Mysterious Sword. In either case, the mentality of moving the body and limbs is the same.

Attacking precipitously is extremely undesirable.[27] Making precipitous attacks or attacks one after another can be accomplished if you have clearly kept your concentration below the waist, and if you have made a complete observation of the situation after the match has begun. It is essential not to be flustered.

RETURNING THE MIND[28]

The frame of mind indicated with this phrase is: if you strike with your sword and think, "I've struck!" the mind that thinks

"I've struck!" will stop right there, just as it is. Because your mind does not return from the place you struck, you will be distracted, struck by the second blow of your opponent, and your initiative will be brought to nothing. With your opponent's second blow, you will be defeated.

Returning the mind means the following: if you have struck a blow, do not leave your mind in the place you struck. Rather, after you have made your strike, turn your mind back and observe your opponent. Having been struck, he will now make a strenuous effort. Having been struck, he will be mortified and insulted, and then become angry. If he gets angry, he will become relentless.

Here, if you are negligent, you will be struck by your opponent. It is best to think of him as an angry boar. If you think, "I struck him," your mind will stay with that thought and you will be negligent. You had best be resolved that when your opponent has been struck, he will rally. Also, once struck, your opponent will quickly become more cautious, and you will not be able to strike him with the same mind with which you struck him before. If you strike at him and miss, he will now take the initiative and strike you.

The significance of "returning your mind" is not to stop your mind where you struck, but to pull it back forcibly to your own self. It is in returning your mind and observing the countenance of your opponent. Or, in its ultimate state of mind, it is in not returning your mind at all, but in unrelentingly striking a second and third time without allowing your opponent so much as a shake of the head. This is what is called "having no space to slip in a single hair."[29] Between your first and second blow, there should be no interval that would allow in even a single hair. This is the mind with which you hit, hit, and hit again.

On the "Dharma battlefield" of Zen questions and answers, even when responding to a single line, the adept answers without the interval that would allow the insertion of a single hair. If you lengthen that interval of time, you will be put in difficult straits. This is the clarity of victory and defeat. And this is again having no space to slip in a single hair.

Striking repeatedly two or three times: this is called the precipitousness of the sword.

- The Mental State of One Expulsion[30]
- The Mental State of Emptiness[31]
- The Mental State of the Firmly-Held Mind[32]

In these mental states, the heart of the One Expulsion is in ridding yourself of a number of things at once. "A number of things" means a number of sicknesses. Sickness means the sickness of the mind. To the extent that they are in the mind, these sicknesses need to be placed together and then lightly tossed away.

In Buddhism, this is called "attachment,"[33] and is very much abhorred. If the mind is attached and stops in one place, you will not see what you are looking at and will suffer unimagined defeat. A stopping of the mind is called sickness. The mind that wraps these various sicknesses up together and tosses them away is called One Expulsion.

Expelling various sicknesses at one time is done so that you don't overlook the One Alone. The One Alone is called Emptiness. This Emptiness is itself a "hidden word" and is transmitted secretly.

"Emptiness" means the mind of your opponent. The mind has no form and no color and is void. The phrase, "To see Emptiness, the One Alone" refers to seeing the mind of your opponent. Buddhism enlightens you to the fact that this mind is Emptiness. Although there are men who preach that mind is Emptiness, the truly enlightened man is rare.

The Chinese characters of the Firmly-Held Mind can be read as "consecrating the mind." Your opponent's mind is consecrated to the hands that grasp the sword. His fists grasp the sword[34] and you should strike them, just as they are, before they move.

The One Expulsion is for the purpose of seeing the place that may or may not move.[35] This is called "a single expulsion of a hundred sicknesses, and not overlooking Emptiness."

Your opponent's mind is in his hands, and is being held up, or consecrated, there. Striking at the place that does not move is called "striking at Emptiness." Emptiness does not move, because it has no form. The significance of striking at Emptiness is that you strike at the place that does not move. This is called Emptiness, and it is the fundamental principle of Buddhism.

Within Emptiness itself, there is a distinction between False

Emptiness[36] and True Emptiness.[37] The first Chinese character in False Emptiness can be read as "lifeless," while the first Chinese character in True Emptiness can be read as "actuality." This being so, False Emptiness is an Emptiness both false and without life, and is given as an example of nothingness. True Emptiness is the Emptiness of actuality, and is therefore the Emptiness of the mind.[38]

The mind has no form and is therefore similar to False Emptiness. But the One Mind is the master of this body, and all your manifold skills are in the mind. The functions and movements of that mind are its activities. When the mind does not move, it is Emptiness. When Emptiness moves, it is mind. When Emptiness moves, it becomes mind, and the hands and feet come into play.

When the fists that grasp the sword do not move, and you quickly strike those fists—that is called "striking at Emptiness."

The Firmly-Held Mind is also the mind that cannot be seen. It is called Emptiness both because it cannot be seen and because it does not move. The mind is consecrated in the hands that grasp the sword, but this cannot be seen. You must strike at the point where the mind consecrated in the hand has not yet moved.

We say that this Emptiness of the mind cannot be seen, and so is nothingness. But if it moves, it does a variety of things: it grasps with the hands, steps with the feet, and accomplishes a variety of wonders. This is the movement and manifestation of this emptiness and this mind.

The enlightenment of this mind is difficult to obtain by looking at books, or to reach by listening to sermons.[39] From times long past, men have written books and given sermons, and their deeds have resembled the Dharma in both the written and spoken word. Still, it is said that those whose Original Mind was enlightened were few.

As man's various skills and wonders are all works of the mind, this mind is in Heaven and Earth as well. This is called the mind of Heaven and Earth. When this mind moves, it brings thunder, lightning, wind, and rain into play. Colorful, unseasonable clouds, snow, and hail blow about, and even chilly rains fall in hot weather, giving man all sorts of afflictions.

This being so, this Emptiness is in Heaven and Earth, and is their master; it is in the body of man, and is that body's master. If you dance, it is the master of the dance; if you perform Noh, it is the master of the Noh. If you use the martial arts, it is the master of the martial arts; if you shoot a firearm, it is the master of the firearm. If you draw a bow, it is the master of the bow; and if you mount a horse, it is the master of the horse.

If this master is perverse, you will be unable to mount the horse and unable to hit the target with the bow or the firearm. If this mind is well-seated, takes its proper position in the body, and resides in its original abode, all Ways will be performed with freedom.

It is important to fix your eyes on this mind at once, and to become enlightened. Though everyone says that they have their eyes opened wide to this mind and can use it well, the men who have their eyes fixed carefully on it are few. Most people's lack of enlightenment will likely be manifested in their bodies. Those who see this and understand, do so quite well.

If a man is enlightened, all of his words and deeds, as well as his physical deportment will be straightforward and right. If he does not carry himself this way, it would be difficult to say that he is enlightened. The Right Mind is called the Original Mind.[40] It is also called the Mind of the Way. The twisted and stained mind is called the deluded mind, or the human mind. The admirable man is the one who is enlightened to his Original Mind and whose actions are in conformity with that Mind.

I do not say these words and speak like this because I have clearly understood my own mind. I speak like this even though it is difficult for me to advance, retreat, move, or be at peace as though I were in accordance with a mind I had made right. Nevertheless, as there *is* a Way, someone must point it out. This said, in the martial arts your actions will come to nothing if you have a mind that is right, but a body and limbs that are not in conformity with that mind.

Though it is possible for your physical movements not to conform with the Way in ordinary life, if you do not grasp the Way in the martial arts, you will not become accomplished. And though you may not stray from this mind in your myriad activities and you may be in conformity with it in your performance of the different arts, it will not translate to things beyond them. When it *does* consciously translate and you act accordingly, you will be called an accomplished[41] man who has arrived at the Principle of all things. When this mind has translated to [just] one art or one ability, a man is called skillful in whatever Way he studies. It would be difficult, however, to call him accomplished.

There is a certain poem:

> *It is the very mind itself*
> *That leads the mind astray;*
> *Of that mind,*
> *Do not be unmindful.*[42]

This can be explained in the following way:

It is the very mind itself. This mind is the distracted mind, the undesirable mind. It misleads the Original Mind.

That leads the mind astray. The mind referred to here is the Original Mind, the one deluded by the distracted mind.

Of that mind. This is the distracted mind.

Do not be unmindful. This refers to the Original Mind, and the line is saying that we should not entrust the Original Mind to the confused mind.[43]

This speaks about truth and delusion.

Our minds contain both the Original Mind and the distracted or deluded mind. If you obtain the Original Mind and are able to conduct yourself in accordance with it, everything will be straightforward and right. But if this Original Mind is covered over, distorted, and sullied by the deluded mind, everything you do will be distorted and soiled.

The Original Mind and the deluded mind are not like black and white, which are easily distinguished when placed side by side. What is called the Original Mind is the original face you had before your mother and father were born,[44] and is without form. It is not born and does not perish. Your form is what is given at birth by your mother and father; but it would be difficult to state that your mind, which has no form, was given birth by them. With man's birth, he is provided with a body.

I have been told that Zen is the sect that transmits this mind. I have likewise heard that there are many men who adhere to something that looks like Zen,[45] whose speech resembles Zen, but who have not entered the True Path. Such are completely different from the Zen Man.

What is called the deluded mind is an impetuous mind, and is self-interested. If you would ask what this impetuousness is, it is activity of the blood.[46] Your blood moves, rises to the top, changes your complexion, and shows your anger.

Again, if what you love is detested by someone else, you will grow angry and resentful. On the other hand, if what you detest is detested in the same way by another, you will rejoice, twist what is wrong, and consider it reasonable. If someone gives you money, you will receive it happily while your face broadens into a smile and reddens with the complexion of the impetuous mind.

In a case like this, wrong is converted into "principle," and all of this is a mind that wells up from our impetuous physical bodies, according to the moment. This is called the deluded or distracted mind. When this occurs, the Original Mind is hidden and becomes the deluded mind,[47] and nothing but undesirable events are manifested.

Thus, a man who understands the Way is respected because he makes his foundation in the Original Mind, and weakens the deluded mind. The man who does not understand the Way acts crookedly. He distorts and muddies his own name because he hides his Original Mind and nurtures the deluded mind.

Although this poem is not a particularly skillful one, it does clearly distinguish the heretical and the correct. With the deluded mind, anything you do is heresy. If this heretical mind is present, you will lose in the martial arts, miss the mark with the bow, fail with the firearm, and be unable to ride a horse. Your performance of Noh will be unsightly, your chanting will be offensive to the ear, and what you say will only manifest your misunderstanding. Everything you do will be a deviation.

If you are in conformity with your Original Mind, everything should turn out well.

If you devise a falsehood, but then deny it, that falsehood will soon become apparent because it was devised with the deluded mind. If your mind is truthful, people will recognize it as such in the end, and there will be no need for explanations. The Original Mind does not call for explanations.

The deluded mind is a sickness of the mind.

Expelling this deluded mind is said to be expelling sickness.

If you can expel this sickness, your mind will be free of sickness. This mind free of sickness is the Original Mind.

If you can arrive at this Original Mind, you will be a master of the martial arts.

All things conform to this principle.

ON THE NO-SWORD

The significance of the term No-Sword is not necessarily in having to take the sword of your opponent. Nor does it mean taking your own sword in display and making a name for yourself.

No-Sword means not being cut by another, although you yourself have no sword. Certainly the real meaning does not lie in saying, "Let me demonstrate how I can take this!"

If your opponent does not want his sword taken, you should not insist on trying to take it. No-Sword is also in *not* taking the sword when your opponent has this attitude. A man who is consumed by the thought of not having his sword taken is going to forget the aim of cutting his opponent. And when he thinks only of not having his sword taken, he will probably not cut you.

Not being cut is in itself a victory. Considering it an art to take a man's sword is not the principle here. The practice is one that a man puts to use when he himself has no sword and does not want to be cut.

What is called No-Sword is not the art of taking a man's sword; it is being able to use all implements freely. When you have no sword and want to take your opponent's to use as your own, anything that comes into your hands should be of use. Even if you have only a fan, you should be able to defeat your opponent's sword. No-Sword is precisely this attitude.

When you have no sword but carry a bamboo staff, and your opponent unsheathes a long sword and attacks, you should be able to handle the bamboo staff and take his sword. But even if you do not take his sword, you should be able to restrain him without being cut. This in itself is a victory.

This frame of mind is the fundamental meaning of No-Sword.

No-Sword consists of neither taking your opponent's sword nor cutting him. But if your opponent is clearly trying to cut you, his sword should be taken. From the very beginning, however, the fundamental meaning is not the taking of a sword. It is the clear understanding of distance.

There is a certain space between you and your opponent, and you should know the distance that will keep his sword from striking you. If you have a good grasp of this distance, you will not fear the strike of your opponent's sword; and when you realize that he is going to strike, you can move according to your judgment of that strike.

With No-Sword, you cannot take your opponent's sword when it is not within striking distance of your body; but you can take it when it is within striking range. In taking it, there is a chance that you will be cut.

No-Sword is the expectation of a match when your opponent carries a sword and you yourself have only your hands to use as weapons. A sword is long, your hands are short, and you will be unable to draw close to your opponent without entering a range in which you might be cut. Can you exercise enough judgment to match your hands against the opponent's sword? If so, can you anticipate moving beneath the hilt of the opponent's sword when the blade passes your body, and taking hold of his sword in this manner?

The circumstances are crucial and you must not become entangled with the opponent indiscriminately. Nevertheless, you will likely never be able to take your opponent's sword without drawing close to him.

No-Sword is considered an exclusive secret of our style. Body stances, sword positions, the lay of the location, distance, movement, inner workings, sticking close to the opponent, attack, deception—each of these comes from the thought of No-Sword. Thus, it is our essential vision of this art.

Great Potential, Great Function[48]

There is substance[49] and function in all things. When there is substance, there is function. The bow, for example, is substance;

drawing back, releasing, and hitting, however, are said to be the functions of the bow. The lantern is substance, while its light is function. Water is substance, and moisture is the water's function. The plum tree is substance, while what are called its scent and color are its functions. The sword is substance; cutting and piercing are its functions.

Thus, Potential is substance. Exterior manifestations and the various workings are called Function. Because the plum tree has substance, flowers bloom from that substance, colors appear,[50] and a scent issues forth. Similarly, Potential is within, while its Function acts without; and in this same line, the various stratagems and deceptions, the stances of Attacking and Abiding, and all the various contrivances of change act externally because Potential is ready within. This is called Function.

"Great" is a word of praise; it is used when speaking of the *Daimyojin, Daigongen*, and *Daibosatsu*,[51] and indicates appreciation. Because Great Potential exists, Great Function is manifested.

Zen monks move about with unrestricted freedom, and no matter what they do or say, it all accords with Reason and Principle. This is called both the "Great Supernatural Power" and the "Great Potential, Great Function.

Though it is called Supernatural Power or Supernatural Transformation, it is not a matter of some divine occurrence like a god or demon coming down from the sky and performing wondrous acts. It is simply acting with complete freedom, in all one's actions. The various sword stances, strategies, and deceptions, the handling of all weapons, leaping up, leaping down, taking another's sword with your bare hands, or delivering a kick—all are called Great Function when done with a freedom beyond the ken of normal instruction.[52]

If Potential is not always maintained within, Great Function is unlikely to become manifest.

Even when seated in a room to which you have been invited, you first look up and then to the right and the left to be aware of anything that might fall on you accidentally. When seated by a door or screen, you bear in mind that they may fall down. Or, when in close attendance upon a member of the nobility or a person of high rank, you remain aware that something unexpected may occur. Even in entering or exiting through a gate, you do not fall into inattention. Constantly keeping these things in mind is Potential.

Because this Potential is always within, in case of an emergency you will be capable of some commendable quick action. This is called Great Function.

When this Potential is not mature, however, Function will not be manifested. Potential will mature and Great Function will issue forth if you continually maintain awareness and accumulate effort in all your disciplines. If Potential coagulates or becomes set, there will be no Function. If it matures, it will spread throughout your entire body and Great Function will occur everywhere: in the hands and feet, in the eyes and ears.

The man who has only practiced the martial arts as usual will not be able to raise a hand against a man of Great Potential and Great Function.

Another matter that should be mentioned is "the stare." If glared at by a man of Great Potential, your mind will be arrested by that look, and you are likely to just stand there forgetting that you have a hand with which to draw your sword. If you miss the moment by even the blink of an eye, you will suffer defeat.

When a cat stares at a mouse, the mouse will fall off the rafter. The mouse's attention is caught by the cat's glare, it forgets the very feet that do its walking, and falls. Meeting a man with Great Potential is like a mouse meeting a cat.

As one Zen verse has it, "There is no established rule for clearly manifesting Great Function."[53] "Clearly manifesting" means that the Great Function of a man of Great Potential appears right before your eyes. "There is no established rule" means that a man of this caliber does not in the least adhere to practice and drills. "Rules" means practice, drills, and regulations. Regulations exist in all disciplines, but the man who has reached the deepest principles of his discipline can dispense with them as he pleases. This is complete freedom, and a man of Great Potential and Great Function has freedom beyond the rules.

Potential means having no negligence within, and being in anticipation of all things. If that continually aware Potential congeals or hardens, however, the mind becomes shackled by Potential and loses its freedom. This is because Potential is not yet mature. It becomes mature though continuous effort, spreads throughout the body, and acts with freedom. This is what is called Great Function.

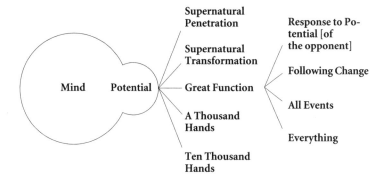

Potential is *ch'i*.[54] It is called potential according to its seat.[55] The mind is the interior, while the *ch'i* is the entrance. Potential is a pivot, much like the pivot of a door. You should understand that if the mind is the master of the body, it is the person seated within. *Ch'i* is the entrance door and permits the mind, as master, to come into play outside. The good or evil of the mind is understood only by this Potential's coming to good or evil after having gone outside. When *ch'i* strictly guards the entrance door, it is called Potential.

A man may push a door on its pivot, go outside and do either good or evil, or even perform some supernatural act. This, however, depends on the thought given to the action while the door was still shut.

Thus, this Potential is of great importance. If Potential acts and goes outside, Great Function is manifested. At any rate, if you think of it as *ch'i*, you will not be wrong. The change in name will depend on the location.

Nevertheless, though one speaks of the "interior" and the "entrance," there are no places inside the body definitely termed as such. Both "interior" and "entrance" are words, and this is how people speak. When you start to speak, it can be called the "entrance;" when you come to your conclusion, it can be called the "interior." But in this case, the locations of interior and entrance are not fixed.

A verse by Manorhata[56] goes:

> The mind follows the ten thousand circumstances
> > and shifts accordingly;
> It is the shifting that is truly undefined.

This verse is a secret of those who practice Zen meditation. It is recorded here because it contains an essential meaning for the martial arts. However, it is probably difficult for anyone who does not practice meditation to understand.

In the martial arts, the "ten thousand circumstances" means the various actions of your opponent, and your mind will shift with each of them.[57] If your opponent lifts his sword, for example, your mind shifts with that sword. If the sword swings to the right, your mind shifts with it; if to the left, your mind follows. This is the meaning of "it follows all circumstances and shifts accordingly."

The phrase "It is the shifting that is truly undefined" is the core of the martial arts. This is probably best understood as the mind that leaves no trace, but "is like the white waves left by a moving boat."[58] They disappear behind, shift forward, and are not detained in the least.

"Undefined" means vague and unseen. This means that the mind is absolutely undetained. If your mind stops in one place, you will be defeated in the martial arts. If it remains in the place to which it has shifted, the results will be merciless.

The mind has neither color nor form, so it cannot be seen by the eye. If it becomes attached and stops, however, it can be observed as it is. It is like white silk: if you dye it red, it becomes red; if you dye it purple, it becomes purple. Imbued with one thing or another, man's mind will also manifest itself and become visible. If it is allowed to become imbued with boys and young men, this will be seen by others in the end.

If thoughts are within, their tints will be manifest without.[59]

If you attentively watch your opponent's movements and your mind stops with them, it is likely that you will be defeated in the martial arts. This verse is quoted to remind you not to stop your mind. I have left out the second stanza and not recorded it here. You will learn it in its entirety when you study zazen. For the martial arts, the first stanza will do.

The martial arts are in accordance with the Buddhist Dharma, and have many points in common with Zen. These include in particular an aversion to attachment and an aversion to being detained by things. It is this that is most to the point. It is essential that one not be detained.

The courtesan of Eguchi responded to the priest Saigyo's[60] poem in this way:

> Having heard you were one
> > who rejected this world,
> My thought is only this:
> > Do not stop your mind
> > in this temporary stay.

In the martial arts, should you not pay special attention to the second half of this verse?

No matter what secret tradition you receive, no matter what technique you use, if your mind is detained by that technique, you will suffer defeat. Your mind should not be detained—whether by the actions of your opponent, by your own actions, or by cutting and thrusting. This is essential.

Abbot Lung-chi[61] once taught the assembled monks and said,

> Do not see the existent pillar as a pillar; do not see the nonexistent pillar as a pillar. Expel Existence and Non-Existence altogether, and make what lies behind them your own.

You should consider these words in regard to all disciplines. I mention them here because a certain wise man[62] noted that they can be thought of in terms of the martial arts.

"The existent pillar and the non-existent pillar" means that just as you can conceive of pillars of existence and non-existence, so can you establish Existence and Non-Existence and Good and Evil in your mind. Placing the concept of Existence in your mind is undesirable, but that of Non-Existence is even more so. To this effect it is said, "Do not see the pillar,"[63] and this is the meaning of "Do not see the pillars of Existence and Non-Existence."

Existence and Non-Existence, Good and Evil, are sicknesses of the mind. If you do not expel these sicknesses from the mind, nothing you do will turn out well. Thus it is said, "Expel Existence and Non-Existence altogether, and make what lies behind them your own." This advocates expelling both Existence and Non-Existence, but continuing to live in the midst of them and advancing to the level of the ultimate.

Even for one accomplished in the Buddhist Dharma, this eye that is independent of Existence and Non-Existence[64] is difficult to obtain.

> You should toss away the Law.
> How much more so the false Law!

The heart of these sentences is that the "Law" means the "True Law of Reality." And even though it may be the "True Law," it should not stop in your mind once you have become enlightened. This is what is said in "You should toss away the Law." After you have become enlightened to the True Law, if you keep it in your mind, it becomes rubbish. This is what is said in

"How much more so the False Law!" You should toss away the True Law. How much more so should a False Law not be kept in your breast!

Action is accomplished with full insight into all principles, lightly throwing those principles off and letting none remain in the mind. It is accomplished by keeping the mind empty, and by keeping it ordinary and nothing special. If you do not reach this level, it will be difficult to call yourself accomplished in the martial arts.

Because our clan is involved in the martial arts, I have spoken of this in conjunction with them; but it should not be restricted to the martial arts alone. All Ways[65] are like this.

In the martial arts it is a sickness if you do not leave the mind of the martial arts behind. In archery it is a sickness if you do not leave the mind of archery behind. If you will only use your ordinary mind and take up the sword or draw the bow, archery will not be difficult and the sword will be used with freedom.

Not being surprised by anything, the ordinary mind will be good for everything. If you lose your ordinary mind, your voice will shake no matter what you are trying to say. If you lose your ordinary mind, your hand will shake when you try to write something in front of others. The ordinary mind is in leaving nothing whatsoever in your breast, lightly tossing off all traces, and leaving the breast empty. This is the ordinary mind.

Those who read the Confucian classics do not understand the principle of the ordinary mind, but are carried away with the word "reverence." The heart of the word "reverence" is not the highest principle. It is a discipline that is only the first or second rung of the ladder.[66]

I have named the first chapter of this book on the martial arts "The Shoe-Presenting Bridge." It is, for the most part, a catalog. The items were transmitted directly from my late father, Tajima no kami Muneyoshi, and his teacher, Kamiizumi Musashi no kami Fujiwara Hidetsuna. This chapter is copied and presented to those who have come to a thorough understanding of those items, and is proof of this transmission.

The second and third chapters are a separate transmission beyond those lessons.[67]

My late father was mindful of this Way his entire life, never letting it slip his mind even while sleeping or eating. For this reason, he understood its mysterious principles. Keeping me at either his right or left, he would habitually discuss its subtleties and lecture on its profundities; and, whenever I heard even the smallest thing, I would respectfully and carefully hold it to my breast.[68]

When I became an adult, I grasped the sword in hand and succeeded to my father's art, but still could not perform with freedom. Eventually I passed the age of "knowing Heaven's decree,"[69] and understood the savor of this Way. Each time I understood one of its principles, I recorded it. As these have accumulated, they have passed through many phases. In the end, they return to the One Mind, the One Mind passes through many things, and these many things are stored in the One Mind. In the end, this is where it is to be found.

Having now written down these observations in two chapters, I combine them with the first for a book of three chapters. This I pass down to my clan.

> *In the Ninth Year of Kan'ei,*[70] *Jinshin in the Chinese chronological cycle,*
> *On a Lucky Day in the Ninth Month—*
>
> *Kamiizumi Musashi no kami Fujiwara Hidetsuna*
> *My late father, Yagyu Tajima no kami Taira Muneyoshi*
> *His son, Yagyu Tajima no kami Taira Munenori*

I have named the second and third chapters of this volume "The Death-Dealing Sword" and "The Life-Giving Sword."[71] At the heart of this work is the idea that the sword that kills people can, on the contrary, become a sword that gives them life. In a chaotic society, many people are killed for no reason. The Death-Dealing Sword is used to bring a chaotic society under control; but once this has been done, cannot that same sword become a Life-Giving Sword? This is why I have given the chapters these names.

AFTERWORD

Munenori and Musashi were by no means the only famous swordsmen to establish styles in the first half of the seventeenth century. By the time of Munenori's death, there were at least two hundred schools of swordsmanship, many in Edo, and most professing to possess the highest learning or deepest secrets of the art. Their approaches ranged dramatically: from Ono no Tadaaki of the Itto-ryu, with its singular emphasis on technique; to Odagiri Ichiiun, whose Mujushin-ryu took a uniquely philosophical approach that considered technique least important; to Munenori and his Yagyu Shinkage-ryu, which sought a middle ground between Zen teachings and technique. But of these, it was Munenori's style that was officially practiced by the shogunate, and which would reach to worlds far beyond Munenori's.

Munenori not only founded an establishment that would secure his clan into the future, but also honored his forebears and their teachers by taking what they had passed on to him and bringing it to perfection. He had been a dutiful son, a prudent parent, and a loyal subject. Thus, the philosophical foundation of Munenori's swordsmanship was in Zen Buddhism, but his social thought lay entirely in Confucianism. This is expressed clearly both in his writings and in his final requests to Iemitsu.

In the face of such a broad spectrum of success then, why the hint of wistfulness expressed in the statue hallowed at the Hotokuji? What lingering regrets might Munenori have had?

Could it be that, despite having brought the Yagyu Shinkage-ryu to unexcelled heights, Munenori regretted that he had never had the opportunity to work out his techniques in the free, wandering life of a *shugyosha*[1] as so many of his contemporaries had done? And what of the savor of those dangerous but free years that he had never tasted? So much of his formative youth had been spent under the aegis of his almost legendary father that he may have sometimes wondered about his own contributions, and where they lay in value compared to those of Sekishusai and Kamiizumi Ise no kami Hidetsuna.

Then there was the specter of Miyamoto Musashi, a loner seeming to have no background at all, and undefeated in over sixty matches. This man, connected to no school or teacher, had beaten and brought on the defection of a number of Munenori's own disciples, including the respected daimyo Hosokawa Tadatoshi. How could this be? Munenori had never had the time or opportunity to meet this eccentric artist/swordsman, as had his nephew in Owari, Yagyu Hyogonosuke. Surely he must have wondered who the man was, and what he was like.

And Hyogonosuke. It was he who had received the direct lineage of the Yagyu Shinkage-ryu from Sekishusai, despite not having been one of Sekishusai's sons. Further, he was teaching only a junior branch of the Tokugawa in the countrified castle-town of Nagoya. Yet matches between the Edo and Owari branches of the school seemed to go in favor of the latter, and it was whispered that Hyogonosuke was perhaps the better swordsman. A formal match between the two men themselves, however, had never taken place, and so the point was moot.

Also cast into the picture was Munenori's wild son, Jubei Mitsuyoshi, who had been officially banished from Edo for thirteen years for some unspecified offense to Iemitsu. Rumor had it (and still has it) that Mitsuyoshi was actually on an intelligence-gathering mission for Iemitsu, once again using the old Yagyu ties to the ninja families of Iga and Koga. Mitsuyoshi himself, however, claimed only to have returned to Yagyu-mura during that time for introspection and perfecting his own sword style. He, too, is said to have gone beyond his father in that art.

Above all, Munenori must have felt from time to time that his very success had become his own prison, as comfortable and honored a place as it may have been. His many positions and responsibilities surely took their toll. We can imagine how he must have enjoyed his leisure during his final six months at Yagyu-mura.

But even this last seemed to end in sadness. Was Munenori called back to Edo upon the fatal illness of Takuan, or did he arrive back only to find that his closest friend and mentor had already passed away? Either way, his own demise only three months later may well have been brought on by loneliness and a broken heart. For all of Munenori's genius, he was not made, as they say, of wood or stone.

Nevertheless, it is Munenori and *Heiho kadensho* that have remained the essential paradigms of the Yagyu Shinkage-ryu for the last three hundred and fifty years. Surely the reader will find something pertaining to himself, his art, and his own approach to the world through a careful contemplation of Munenori's words and a thorough consideration of the discipline and thoughtfulness of his life. Here, to our good fortune, is a signpost to better chart our own understanding and actions.

The wistfulness found in no exact place on this otherwise imposing statue may suggest the branched streams that flow through a man's life, augmenting and nourishing the greater current as it perseveres on its way. Munenori navigated that current with strength, skill, and intelligence that still inspire us today.

—WILLIAM SCOTT WILSON

ILLUSTRATED CATALOG OF THE SHINKAGE-RYU MARTIAL ARTS

Produced by Yagyu Sekishusai and presented to his friend, Noh actor Konparu Shichiro Ujikatsu, in 1601. The accompanying descriptions were written by Matsudaira Nobusada—accomplished swordsman of the Yagyu Shinkage-ryu[1]—in 1707 at the request of Ujikatsu's descendents.

One Cut, Two Halves

When your opponent takes the *chudan* stance, aiming the tip of his sword at your eyes, drop your sword back to the right like a wheel, advance your left foot, and cock your left knee slightly. Your body should be at an oblique angle to your opponent. Draw the sword slowly but surely to the front while fixing your eyes. When the hips seem set for an attack and your opponent strikes at your left shoulder, release the fixation of your eyes, drop your fist to your knee, and extend your left elbow with certainty and deflect his blow. As he raises his sword to strike, step forward with your right foot, open your stance to the rear and cut his left wrist. An oral transmission.

Cutting Through Nails, Slicing Through Steel

When your opponent faces you directly, taking the *jodan* stance, and you take the same, advance to where the two swords cross about three inches from the tips. If your opponent strikes at your right shoulder from the inside, disengage your sword and step forward with the left foot. Face your opponent obliquely and release the fixation of the eyes. As he raises his sword to strike, step forward with your right foot, and strike with a sweeping cut from below. As you bring your sword sideways, lower it immediately. If he raises his sword, cut his left wrist as above. An oral transmission.

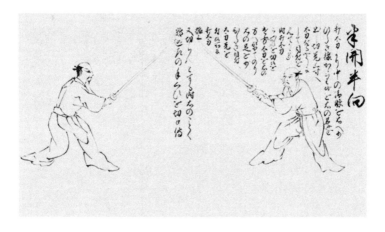

Half-Open, Half-Opposed

Your opponent takes a *chudan* stance with the point of his sword directed at your face and then moves the sword slightly to the right. Step forward with your right foot, move as though to cross his sword about three inches from the tip, and fix your eyes. When your opponent strikes at your fists, move your sword to the right and step slightly to the right with your right foot, thrusting the tip of your sword at the point where you had fixed your eyes. If your opponent raises his sword and makes to strike at you again, step forward as above and cut his wrists. An oral transmission.

*

Circling Right, Turning Left

When your opponent takes a direct *jodan* posture and advances to strike forcefully, cross swords and make to cut at his wrists, circling one or two steps to the left. As you do so, step slightly to the left with your left foot, lower the tip of your sword a little, and dodge his blow. An oral transmission.

Again, if your opponent attacks somewhat weakly, forcefully strike the tip of his sword and then join with him a second time. Take the mental attitude of slightly drawing back the tip of your sword, and wait. Fix your eyes well. When your opponent steps forward with his right foot and strikes at your fists, step forward with your left foot and strike by extending both hands quickly. An oral tradition.

Long and Short, One and the Same

When your opponent takes a direct *chudan* stance, and your swords are a bit too far apart, he may attack only to assess your designs. As you join the rhythm of his sword, advance your left foot as though to move to the right, dropping your sword to *gedan*. Fixing your eyes well, strike a decisive blow, but remain alert. An oral transmission.

In our land, the martial arts began with the gods Izanagi and Izanami.[2] Izanagi took up some leafy willow, and Izanami opposed him with a branch of bamboo. Later, this was brought to Amaterasu Omikami,[3] and she took great interest in this Way. The heavenly gods introduced it to the earthly gods, the earthly gods introduced it to the emperors, and from the emperors it was received by innumerable people. By means of the three-foot sword, rebellions were quelled and our nation was saved. How could this have been in vain? Those who study it must make great effort!

THE NINE ITEMS

Certain Victory

When your opponent displays a *jodan* stance, take the *yin* position.[4]
As he makes to strike your fists with the tip of his sword, draw your
right foot out to the rear and bring your sword down to strike. Take
a stance with your two hands forming a triangle and wait. Just as your
opponent strikes at your hands from above, step slightly out with your
right foot and defeat him by striking his hands from beneath. Again,
when striking swiftly from above, follow through by sweeping up
from below. Aim your sword between his hands, then cut his fists
with a downward sweep. To finish him off, when he pushes directly
forward, strike downward, wait, brush away his sword with an upward
stroke, and defeat him by going right over him. An oral transmission.

Crosswind

When your opponent displays a *jodan* posture, take the usual *yin* position, quickly leap to his left, and strike sideways at his shoulder. Draw the sword to your left and withdraw slightly. Fix your eyes well and, just when he strikes with an upward blow, step forward with your left foot, cut through his two hands, and hold back. An oral transmission.

Cross-Shaped Swords

When your opponent has taken a *jodan* position and is assessing your designs, take up a similar stance and do the same. With this balanced rhythm, step to the right and then step in with your left foot. With the swords forming a triangle, thrust out both hands and fix your eyes. When your opponent steps into the space between the two of you, deflect the tip of his sword. If he strikes downward, step outward and cut his right fist. Do not tarry here, but when you cut from above, draw back, then strike at an angle, making a sweeping cut of his two arms. An oral transmission.

Reconciliation

When your opponent has taken the *chudan* stance with the tip of his sword directed at your face, approach him as if in *gedan*, thrust out your sword, step forward with your right foot, open your stance, and defeat him by pressing in. An oral transmission.

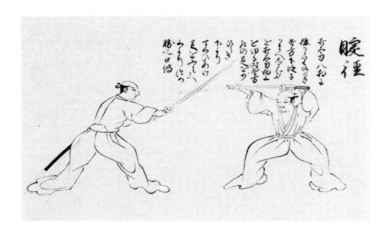

Shortcut

When your opponent takes the *hasso* posture,[5] attack from a *gedan* posture. As he strikes from directly above, move your left foot slightly to the outside, dip up from below, shift from one foot to the other, and defeat him by pressing in and deflecting him from above. An oral transmission.

Fine Stifling[6]

As your opponent takes a stance with his sword held over his right knee, take a *gedan* stance and cross swords about three inches below their tips. As he raises his sword to draw you in, defeat him by stepping in with your left foot and deflecting him at chest level. An oral transmission.

Broad Stifling

When your opponent comes at your directly from above and thrusts straight forward, stabbing along his line of sight, cross swords about three inches below the tips and take similar action. As you begin, avoid his sword by bringing yours upward. In that rhythm, lift your hands slightly, cut him down, and hold back. An oral transmission.

Eight-Layered Fence

When your opponent has taken a direct *jodan* stance, take the *hasso* position. He will fix his eyes on you and advance toward that point. Adjust your stance by stepping back slightly with your right foot and strike from above. As your opponent steps forward to strike, push in close and cut both of his arms. An oral transmission.

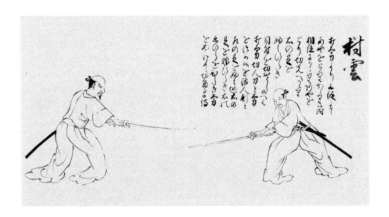

Billowing Clouds

When your opponent takes a *jodan* stance and is testing your designs, take the same position and test his plans. Advance toward the tip of his sword, slightly open your stance with your right foot and strike downward at the point where you have fixed your eyes. As your opponent pushes forward with his sword in position (the Death-Dealing Sword), take the *gedan* position (the Life-Giving Sword) and step forward with your left foot. Step out with your right foot broadening your stance, evade his sword, strike, and hold back. An oral transmission.

TENGU'S SELECTION

Korinbo[7]

Ranko (乱甲): Both opponent and practitioner take a *jodan* stance. The opponent attacks and the practitioner meets him with the same, stepping forward with his right foot and striking. As the opponent steps in and strikes, the practitioner opens to the left, steps in with the right foot, cuts the opponent's fists, and holds back. An oral transmission.

Fugenbo

Noritachi (乗太刀): Both opponent and practitioner test the other's designs. As the opponent attacks, the practitioner leaps up, almost as though floating, and engages the opponent's sword from above. When the opponent meets this by wheeling his sword and pulling back, the practitioner stifles the move, strikes, and holds back. An oral transmission.

Tarobo

Komurakumo (小村雲): Your opponent takes up a direct *chudan* position, tests your designs, and steps forward. As he strikes at your fists, move your entire body, cut up from below, and hold back. An oral transmission.

Eiibo

Kiritsume (切詰): Both men take a direct *chudan* stance and test each other's designs. As your opponent steps forward and strikes at your fists, open to the right, step forward, and cut his fists.

Chiraten

Korandome (虎乱留): Your opponent carries two swords—a short sword in his extended left hand and a sword in his right hand which is in the *chudan* wheel. Fix your eyes at the tip of his sword, use the "Manipulating Two Eyes," and, as he strikes, cut him down and hold back. An oral transmission.

Karanbo

Subete koran uchimonodome (全虎乱打物留): Your opponent holds a
sword in his left hand and a short sword in his right. His stance is the
same as above and he advances smoothly. Make your sword and body
one, make a shield of your fists, and strike. Without a moment's interval, attack smoothly. The initial strike should go toward his body; attack as though far away. An oral transmission.

To first cut down through the *shuriken* from an unmoving posture
is called the opening strike. What is important is not the cutting
down, but how the sword is arrayed. There are many oral traditions
about this.

Shutokubo

Kissaskizume (切先詰): Your opponent is in direct *jodan* and testing your designs. You deflect the tip of his sword with a Three Rhythms (三調子), strike, and hold back. An oral transmission.

Konpirabo

In no kasumi: When your opponent takes up the *in no kasumi* stance, you do the same. When at the first count his sword is at his side and at the second count striking, extend your sword at length and with quick footwork defeat him by stifling his blow. An oral transmission.

This is also called the *hashigaeshi* (橋返) and the *toutoukiri* (とうとう切). When meeting two people on a narrow path and being hemmed in both in front and back, it is called *yoshi* (吉). An oral transmission.

Concomitant Cutting, Riotous Cutting

When your opponent attacks, taking a *yin* posture, turn your body to him diagonally, put your left hand forward on the hilt like a misty haze, and hold your sword out to the side. Take a gently inclined stance with your head in line with your sword. When your opponent strikes from above, do a spinning strike that will cut down on his wrists. If he tries to sweep your sword to the side, you will defeat him by swinging your sword both from above and below. This is called Concomitant Cutting, Riotous Cutting. An oral transmission.

Matchless Sword

When your opponent attacks with the posture cited above, meet his eyes about three inches from the tip of your sword, and then lower the sword. Assume a *gedan* position, step forward with your right foot, and open your stance with the other foot to the rear. Fix your eyes and, when he brings his sword down, bring your sword resolutely up from beneath, cut him, and hold back. An oral transmission.

The Life-Giving Sword

Your opponent extends his right foot and lowers his sword in front. You do the same, consider the Moon on Water, and fix your eyes. When you set a contrary rhythm and cause him to strike, strike, and hold back. As above, advancing and retreating numerous times is important. An oral transmission.

The Highest
The Secret Principle
The Mysterious Sword

The Highest is when your opponent attacks from a direct *chudan* position, swords are crossed, and you wish to correct the situation. Perceiving this to be moment of crisis, you abandon everything and strike him down. An oral transmission.

The Secret Principle is when your opponent takes a direct *chudan* position, wields his sword like a mythical lion, and attacks smoothly and without any hesitation. Take up the posture of the Sword, step out with your right foot, and take up a lower position by kneeling with the left foot extended. Let him pass by and defeat him by striking him from the rear. An oral transmission.

The Mysterious Sword is when your opponent takes up the Sword stance and you do the same. As you attack smoothly, he will open up, trying to avoid you with the Secret Principle. Turn with him, pressing your sword across the broad part of his chest, step in between his legs with your left foot, bring your knees against his, and flatten him by pushing him down. An oral transmission.

SOURCES QUOTED IN TEXT

A number of notes have been attached to the text for purposes of either clarification or engaging the further interest of the reader. The following is a list of the Japanese sources most quoted and their authors as recognized by most scholars. The reader will have noticed that the majority of these quotes are from works written by Munenori's son, Mitsuyoshi, or Munenori's friend, Takuan Soho.

The list is given in alphabetical order.

WORK	AUTHOR
Fudochi shinmyoroku (不動智神妙録)	Takuan Soho
Fushikaden (風姿花伝)	Kanze Motokiyo
Himonshu (胐聞集)	Yagyu Mitsuyoshi
Heiho e-mokuroku (兵法絵目録)	Yagyu Sekishusai Muneyoshi
Heiho sesso kokoromochi (兵法截相心持)	Yagyu Munenori
Motsujimi shudan kudensho (没慈味手段口伝書)	Yagyu Sekishusai Muneyoshi
Musashino (武蔵野)	Yagyu Mitsuyoshi
Shinkage-ryu heihosho (新陰流兵法書)	Yagyu Munenori
Shinkage-ryu heiho kokoromochi (兵法新陰流心持)	Yagyu Munenori
Taiaki (太阿記)	Takuan Soho
Tsuki no sho (月之抄)	Yagyu Mitsuyoshi

BIBLIOGRAPHY

WORKS IN JAPANESE

Kaku, Kozo. *Miyamoto Musashi jiten*. Tokyo: Tokyo-do Shuppansha, 2001.

Kanaya, Osamu. *Lao Tzu*. Tokyo: Kodansha, 1997.

Kuwabara, Hiroshi, ed. *Saigyo monogatari*. Tokyo: Kodansha, 1981.

Shimada, Kenji, ed. *Daigaku/Chuyo*. Tokyo: Asahi Shinbunsha, 1967.

Takuan Soho. *Fudochi shinmyoroku*. Ikeda Satoshi, ed. Tokyo: Tokuma Shoten, 1940.

Tsumoto, Akira. *Nihon kenkaku retsuden*. Tokyo: Kodansha, 1987.

Watatani, Kiyoshi and Yamada Tadashi, eds. *Bugei ryuha daijiten*. Tokyo: Tokyo Kopii Shuppanbu, 1978.

Yagyu, Jubei Mitsuyoshi. *Tsuki no sho*. Annotated by Imamura Yoshio. Sanjo-shi: Nojima Shuppan, 1971.

Yagyu, Munenaga. *Shoden shinkage-ryu*. Tokyo: Kodansha, 1957.

Yagyu, Munenori. *Heiho kadensho*. Annotated by Watanabe Ichiro. Tokyo: Iwanami Shoten, 1985.

Yamaoka, Sohachi. *Yagyu Sekishusai*. Tokyo: Kodansha, 1987.

Yoshida, Yutaka, ed. *Budo hidensho*. Tokyo: Tokuma Shoten, 1968.

WORKS IN ENGLISH

Blyth, R. H. *Zen and Zen Classics,* vol. 4, *Mumonkan.* Tokyo: Hokuseido Press, 1966.

Friday, Karl F., and Seki Humitake. *Legacy of the Sword.* Honolulu: University of Hawai'i Press, 1997.

Kiyota, Minoru. *Kendo.* Boston: Shambhala Publications, 1995.

Lowry, Dave. *Bokken: Art of the Japanese Sword.* Santa Clarita, California: Ohara Publications, 1986.

Sansom, George. *A History of Japan, 1615–1867.* Stanford: Stanford University Press, 1963.

Skoss, Diane, ed. *Koryu Bujutsu.* Berkeley Heights: Koryu Books, 1997.

Sugawara, Makoto. *Lives of Master Swordsmen.* Tokyo: The East Publications, 1985.

Suzuki, Daisetz T. *Zen and Japanese Culture.* New York: Bollingen Foundation, 1959.

Takuan Soho. *The Unfettered Mind.* Trans. by William Scott Wilson. Boston: Shambhala Publications, 2012.

Tanaka, Fumon. *Samurai Fighting Arts.* Tokyo: Kodansha International, 2003.

NOTES

Footnotes written by Ichiro Watanabe, except those marked "TRANS.," which have been added by translator William Scott Wilson. (All notes to the Introduction, Afterword, and Catalog, however, are by William Scott Wilson.)

INTRODUCTION

1. It may have been quite surprising to see Shigenari in this role, since his father had been ordered some time before to commit *harakiri* by the Toyotomi.

2. *Ichi no tachi*; *hitotsu no tachi* (一刀).

3. "Everyday mind." *Heijoshin* (平常心).

4. Moviegoers will recognize this episode from the beginning of Akira Kurosawa's *Seven Samurai*.

5. *Inka* (印可). A certificate of achievement awarded by a master to his disciple.

6. Fiefs and stipends were awarded in rice, the standard measurement for which was the *koku*, about five bushels.

7. The Yagyu Shinkage-ryu is permeated by Mikkyo Buddhism, and many of its rites are based on those sects (Tendai and Shingon) even today.

Indeed, the agreement that Ieyasu made with Sekishusai was signed under the guarantee of Marishiten—a Mikkyo Buddhist deity whose mantra and mudra, if properly performed, are said to provide a warrior with invisibility.

8. Dream. *Yume* (夢).

9. A shout that can voice approval, disapproval, or—more often—transcendence of concepts altogether. Used by accomplished Zen priests to shock a monk into some inexpressible insight (or sometimes, it seems, just for the fun of it).

10. Shinkage-ryu in this case is written 神陰流.

11. *Kenzen ichinyo* (剣禅一如) means that the way of the sword and the way of Zen are one. This concept is central to Munenori's teachings.

12. No-Self. *Muga* (無我).

13. During Munenori's time, many people practiced the chanting and even the dances of Noh; this pastime was one of the marks of a cultured person. Takuan likely knew a few Noh chants himself, but Munenori may have demonstrated his ability a little too often, in the priest's eyes.

HEIHO KADENSHO (THE LIFE-GIVING SWORD)
THE SHOE-PRESENTING BRIDGE

1. This title, "The Shoe-Presenting Bridge," is a reference to a story in *Shih chi*, or *The Aristocratic Ancestry of the Marquis of Liu, Chang Liang*, written by Ssu-ma Ch'ien (145–90 B.C.E.) during the Han Dynasty in China. The story is as follows:

> Once Chang Liang was taking a leisurely walk near an earthen bridge in Hsia-p'ei. An old man wearing shabby clothing came up and purposely dropped his shoe over the bridge. Turning to Chang Liang, the old man said, "Go down there and bring me back my shoe, youngster." Chang Liang was shocked and considered giving the old man a pounding, but out of consideration for the fellow's advanced age, he suppressed his feelings, descended the embankment, and brought back the shoe.
>
> The old man then said, "Put the shoe on my foot!" And since he had already brought back the shoe, Chang Liang knelt to put it on

the old man. After the latter had put out his foot and been fitted with the shoe, he laughed and walked off. Chang Liang was extraordinarily surprised, and watched him walk away.

After walking about four hundred yards, the old man turned around and came back. "It would be worth teaching you something, youngster," he said. "Meet me here at dawn after five days." Although he thought this rather strange, Chang Liang knelt and consented to do so.

When Chang Liang went out at dawn five days later, the old man was already there and in a bad temper. "How shameful that you would make a promise to an old man and then be late!" he said. "Go away, and come back to meet me at dawn after five more days."

Five days later, Chang Liang set out as the roosters were crowing, but the old man had arrived already and was once again angry. "What is this tardiness! Go home!" And then, "One more time, come at dawn in five days."

Five days later, Chang Liang set out before midnight. After a short while, the old man came up and said happily, "This is the way it should be!" Taking out a book, he said, "If you read this, you will likely become the teacher of kings. After ten years, you will prosper; and in thirteen years you will meet me again, youngster. I will be the yellow rock at the foot of Mount Ku-ch'eng in northern Ch'i."

Saying nothing more, he left and was never seen again.

When dawn broke, Chang Liang looked at the book and saw that it was *The Martial Art of the Grand Duke Wang Lü Shang*. Chang Liang valued this book highly and, studying it constantly, committed it to memory.

Chang Liang became an extraordinary tactician and was eventually employed by Kao-tsu, emperor of China. Munenori seems to have alluded to this story in the title in deference to Kamiizumi Ise no kami Hidetsuna, the founder of Shinkage-ryu, whom he seems to equate with the old man, and to Sekishusai Muneyoshi, Munenori's father, who received Kamiizumi's teaching at the age of thirty-five and spent the next forty years of his life establishing the principles of that school. Munenori would seem to revere his father as a Chang Liang, and hints that his own book may be regarded as akin to *The Martial Art of the Grand Duke Wamg Lü Shang*.
—TRANS.

2. This refers to the Three Learnings of Buddhism: Precepts, Meditation, and

Wisdom. In the case of the martial arts, the Three Learnings are the three essentials for carrying the body freely, and are the great prerequisites for disciplined study.

3. These are all related to body posture.

> Whether striking or parrying, these must not be forgotten. When one is a beginner, they are intended to correct strain from incorrect body posture. It is the same as correcting unevenness in a bow. . . .
>
> If you know your body well, knowing strain is knowing yourself. If you think only of what's in front of you, you will forget about straining your body . . . correcting strain is the first stage of understanding in knowing yourself.　　　　　　　　　　　　　　*—Himonshu*

4. This alludes to the Zen Buddhist phrase, "instantaneously cutting through the two views of Existence and Non-Existence," and to the famous sixty-third case of the *Pi Yen Lu*, a collection of Zen koans compiled in twelfth-century China, in which a Zen priest very un-Buddhistically cuts a cat in two with utter decisiveness. The other four titles are said to be from the same collection.

5. In his *Tsuki no sho*, Yagyu Mitsuyoshi instructs readers to "consider these five essential in maintaining a stance. They are the mental attitudes for Abiding."

6. These are said to be the nine practices that Kamiizumi Ise no kami Hide-tsuna reorganized and adapted for the Shinkage-ryu. He selected the nine specifically from the practices he had mastered that expressed the deepest principles of the Shindo-ryu and other styles of the time.

7. In February of 1601, Sekishusai gave an illustrated scroll that was essentially a sword manual to his friend, Noh actor Konparu Shichiro Ujikatsu. The techniques were illustrated with *tengu*—mythical half-human, half-bestial characters with long noses and wings—who were held to be master swordsmen. This short manual, entitled *Illustrated Catalog of the Shinkage-ryu Martial Arts* (*Shinkage-ryu heiho e-mokuroku* 新陰流兵法絵目録), includes illustrations of the Five Stances, the Nine Items, and the following Six Techniques. [The complete manual can be found on pages 77–102 of this book.]

8. Considered to be the deepest principles of the Shinkage-ryu.

9. The postures of Concomitant Cutting and Riotous Cutting can be defeated by the Matchless Sword. That in turn can be defeated by the Life-Giving Sword. The Life-Giving Sword will be defeated by Elevation, and Elevation will be defeated by the Secret Principle. The Secret Principle will be defeated by the Sword of Mystery. This is the ultimate. It is called the Sword of Mystery because it is said that there is nothing beyond it. From this point, the mental attitudes of the martial arts are said to all be in the ultimate of One Mind.

—*Musashino*

10. Battle headquarters. Heavy curtains enclosing an area near the battle field where the generals could plan strategy in private. —TRANS.

11. From *Han shu* (漢書) or *History of the Former Han*, compiled by Pan Ku (32–92 C.E.).

12. Up to this point, the word "stratagem" has been *hakarigoto* (策): a scheme, contrivance, design, or stratagem. The word is probably based on the root meaning of *hakaru* (策る), which is to balance or measure. Here, however, Munenori uses the word *hyori* (表裏), which is variously defined as double-dealing, dishonesty, or deception. Written with the Chinese character for "inside" followed by that for "outside," it carries the sense of showing one thing on the surface, while having something else in mind. Munenori declares that this *hyori* is the basis of the martial arts. —TRANS.

13. In his *Musashino*, Yagyu Mitsuyoshi notes that *jo* (序) is described as the combat before the attack, *ha* (破) as the attack itself, and *kyu* (急) as the responding blow of each contestant. In modern kendo practice in the English-speaking world, these terms are generally left untranslated, and that tradition will be followed here as well from this point. —TRANS.

14. Exactly how Munenori taught these three basic stances is not clear, but in modern kendo they are: *jodan*—the sword held above the forehead, ready to strike at the opponent's head; *chudan*—the sword held ready to thrust at the opponent's throat or chest; and *gedan*—the sword tilted forward and down. —TRANS.

15. As in the music accompanying Noh drama, with which Munenori was very familiar. —TRANS.

16. Properly, Huang Shih-kung, the old man in the story. —TRANS.

17. See Note 1 above.

THE DEATH-DEALING SWORD

1. Paraphrase of the *Tao Te Ching*, Chapter 31:

> Fine weapons are instruments of ill omen.
> All things seem to hate them.
> Therefore the man of the Way avoids them. . . .
> Weapons are instruments of ill omen,
> And are not those of the Gentleman.
> He uses them only when it cannot be helped.
> He puts tranquillity and indifference at the fore,
> And does not glorify victory.

2. Takuan, in the *Takuan sho*, understood this Chinese character, *katsu* (活) as *yomigaeru* (蘇), meaning "resuscitate" or "revive."

3. The word used here is *ho* (法), which can be variously understood as "law," "method," "art," or "Dharma." It is also one of the two characters used to write "martial art" (*heiho* or *hyoho* 兵法), however, and this would seem to be the concept Munenori had in mind.   —TRANS.

4. Compared to the "large" martial art practiced by army generals in battle.

5. *Taiki taiyo* (大機大用). A phrase used in Zen Buddhist philosophy. Briefly, it means true Function manifested from true Principle. This can only be demonstrated when practice and principle are internalized and at the same time transcended or "forgotten."

6. The phrase here is *shuji shuriken no umu o miru* (手字種利剣の有無を見る), or "seeing into the existence and non-existence of *shuji shuriken*."

   Shuji refers to meeting your opponent's sword in a cross pattern (*ju* 十) no matter how he may strike; it is a practice done to keep from being struck. It is said that if you meet the opponent's sword in a cross pattern, he will be unable to strike you. *Shuriken* is the underside of his hand [technique]; when you see this underside, you will defeat him. This is called the victory of existence and non-existence. It is said that when you can see the existent in the non-existent, you will win. —*Himonshu*

7. In other words, to have his disciples know and continue to transmit the real swordsmanship, and not have it diluted by making it public.

   Knowing the Hidden Flower. If it is hidden, it becomes a flower. If it is not hidden, it will likely not become a flower. Knowing one's self is the essential flower. In all things, in all Ways, the reason for keeping things secret within the hereditary line is that great performance depends on this secret.

The methods used in the Way of War are an example of this. The schemes, plans, and unexpected methods of a great general will defeat even a strong enemy. This is because the losing side will be confused by rare principles and be destroyed, is it not? . . .

In all things, in all Ways, there is a principle of victory in combat. Thus, in our hereditary line, we keep some things secret.

—*Fushikaden*

8. One of the Confucian Four Books. It deals with self-cultivation.

—TRANS.

9. *Chichi kakubutsu* (致知格物). The passage in which this appears in *The Great Learning* is *Yokusei kiisha, senchi kichi, chichi zai kakubutsu* (欲誠其意者、先致其知、致知在格物). "Those who wish to make their wills sincere, first extend their knowledge. Extending knowledge is in extending it to all things." This is one of the most difficult and most often discussed lines in Confucian philosophy, and any number of scholars have interpreted it differently over the millennia. Munenori here tries his own hand at interpreting it, "extending" it to the martial arts. I have generally followed Shimada's interpretation in translating the phrase. —TRANS.

10. As the beginner knows nothing about either his body posture or the positioning of his sword, his mind does not stop anywhere within him. If a man strikes at him with the sword, he simply meets the attack without anything in mind.

As he studies various things and is taught the diverse ways of how to take a stance, the manner of grasping his sword and where to put his mind, his mind stops in many places. Now if he wants to strike at an opponent, he is extraordinarily discomforted. Later, as days pass and time accumulates, in accordance with his practice, neither the postures of his body nor the ways of grasping the sword are weighed in his mind. His mind simply becomes as it was in the beginning when he knew nothing, and had yet to be taught anything at all. In this one can see the way in which the beginning is the same as the end ... —*Fudochishinmyoroku*

11. Pronounced *ki* in Sino-Japanese. The word can be translated any number

of ways—including spirit, mind, soul, and intention—but Munenori's meaning seems to come closest to what we understand as *ki/ch'i* today through our exposure to kung fu and aikido. The reader, however, should be aware of the other meanings and nuances.　　　　　—TRANS.

12.　　Deception is hidden; it is the mind that takes in another.—*Tsuki no sho*

13.　　It is essential that the false becomes truth.　　　　—*Tsuki no sho*

14. In Sanskrit, *upaya*. The Buddha realized that the Dharma would not be understood on the basis of just one explanation, by people with different capacities. Thus he devised various "expedient means" and expounded provisional truths so that all might understand. Each level of truth, however, was designed to lead listeners to the deepest truth of all.　—TRANS.

15. No-Sword, or *muto* (無刀): The technique, perfected by Munenori's father, Sekishusai, of clasping the opponent's sword with one's bare hands as it strikes downward.　　　　　　　　　　　—TRANS.

16. "Grasping the Opportunity." *Kizen* (機前). The complete Zen phrase is *Ki imada hassezaru izen* (機 未 発 以 前), which, for Munenori, means roughly, "Establish your initiative even before your opponent's concept has had a chance to develop or move. This will break his spirit and lead your design to fruition." The Chinese character *ki* [機; note the difference between this and the *ki* of Note 11 above] has been taken to mean a number of things in Chinese and Zen philosophies, and its basic meanings are as broad as "moving power" and "opportunity." Munenori seems to accept both, according to context. Once again, the reader is advised to keep both meanings in mind.　　　　　　　　　　　—TRANS.

17. "The moving power of Zen."—*Zenki* (禅機).

18.　　One should carefully observe and know [the opponent's] words, complexion, appearance, pretences, attitudes and habits.　　—*Tsuki no sho*

19.　　To transcend the fundamental first blow is to act on your very first single thought just as it is. This is called taking the victory by the first blow of the first blow [or the initial initiative].　　—*Tsuki no sho*

20. Observing the functions of the opponent's fists as he grasps the handle of his sword.

21. Observing the pattern of the stretch and fold of the elbows. This fixing of the eyes is used when the opponent has taken up the *jodan* position. The right elbow is called the "peak" and the left elbow, the "valley."

22. Fixing the eyes between the top of the shoulders and the chest. This is used when the opponent's Two Stars and Peak and Valley are obscured.

23. This is performed to avoid the direct force of an opponent's attack.

24. This seems to have been a way to avoid striking and being struck at the same time. The meaning of Bead Tree (*Melia azederach*) is obscure, but it may be an allusion to the "Bead Tree Board," or *sendan no ita* (栴檀の板), a plank set from the shoulders across the chest, protecting the lacing connecting the chest armor to the back.

25. These terms—*tsuke*, *kake*, and *narai*—do not invite anything other than approximate translation. In the text, Munenori has written them in the *kana* syllabary rather than in Chinese characters, and the words themselves are quite broad in meaning. To make matters even less clear, Munenori offers no other information than the broad discussion that follows. The reader must keep in mind that much of *Heiho kadensho* was a prompt, reminding the student of what he had already learned in sessions with the teacher.   —TRANS.

26.   A turning point in the opponent's mind—whether it be for an advance, a retreat, or a turn—is called a change, or *iro* (色, literally, "color"). It is important to apply yourself to that change. . . . You cannot reach the level of the practice of following change by your own efforts. You must leave things up to your opponent.   —*Himonshu*

27.   The movement of Two Stars is called Change.   —*Tsuki no sho*

28. "Manipulating two eyes." *Futatsumetsukai* (二目遣い): a term generally used in Noh drama.

29. *Chugan* (偸眼). Looking askance; pretending not to look. Stealing a look.

30. In Japanese, the *atebyoshi* (当拍子), *tsukebyoshi* (付拍子), and *koebyoshi* (越拍子). Sekishusai mentioned these to Noh actor Konparu Shichiro Ujikatsu in *The Illustrated Catalog of the Shinkage-ryu Martial Arts* (see also Note 7, "The Shoe-Presenting Bridge").

31. It is very undesirable for mind, gesture and attack to come together at one time.   —*Himonshu*

32. No-Beat is observing during a strike, observing during an attack, and in any case, observing an observance. It is an action I take to scatter the opponent's mind.   —*Musashino*

33. Yelling and swinging your sword in large gestures is called a Broad Rhythm. . . . A Broad Rhythm is the heart of an attack. Make it big, but keep the mind light.   —*Tsuki no sho*

34. Celerity following the action of fixing the eyes is called Short Rhythm. It is used when your opponent is attacking in small strokes and you cannot take his rhythm . . . Short Rhythm is a fast and detailed mind.
                                                   —*Tsuki no sho*

35. An immediate counter-blow delivered just as the opponent strikes.

36. Defeating an opponent by advancing three inches inside the points of the two opposing swords.

37. Drawing up close to an opponent's body.

38. Checking the space between the elbows when the opponent his holding his sword in *jodan*.

39. The space between the right and left hands as they grip the sword (refer back to the chapter, "The Shoe-Presenting Bridge").

40. The interval between the feet that are furthest forward of the two opponents.

41. My father said that this is the very height of victory, and the ultimate of the martial arts. All the many practices are for the purpose of reaching this point. If you reach this point, every single practice will no longer exist. . . . If you will put your mind into your opponent, the first one who thinks during the match will win. . . . Do not consider existence or non-existence. Simply the person with the first fast thought will win with an Initial Initiative. . . . The mind is the foundation of all thoughts, so the mind is initial. The mind is prior. The very first thought is the initial act. Therefore it is the initiating initiative. This is the ultimate. The very first thought is the foundation of all acts.
                                                   —*Tsuki no sho*

42. Look carefully with Manipulating Two Eyes; your opponent should have a preferred location. Flush out that preferred location directly, make your opponent strike, and defeat him. —*Tsuki no sho*

43. Maintaining total mindfulness regardless of circumstances. To be completely without negligence.

   Whether you defeat your opponent, miss your target, or are preparing yourself; whether you retreat or attack . . . always stay mindful and suffer yourself no negligence in keeping your eyes fixed. This is of the first importance. —*Tsuki no sho*

44. A foot and a half is considered the margin between the tips of the shoulders. Possibly a technique for striking at the opponent's head after missing with a prior stroke.

   The distance between the tips of your right and left shoulders is naturally a foot and a half. If your sword misses that area of the body, strike at your opponent's neck with your short sword. —*Tsuki no sho*

45. In this practice you strictly pacify your mind as you come within three feet of your opponent. Your state of mind should be such that you can hear the faint sound of wind or the flow of a river. —*Tsuki no sho*

   If your attack is rough, you will surely be defeated.

   Scattered flowers

   fall on moss

   without a sound.

   Falling flowers

   can be heard

   deep in the mountains.

   —*Himonshu*

46. The Way of the martial arts is in deception. *Hei wa kido nari* (兵者詭道也)— *Sun Tzu*, I, 8

47. The use of the martial arts does not in rely on my opponent's not coming; it relies on the fact that I am waiting for him. It does not rely on my opponent's not attacking; it relies on my being unassailable.
   —*Sun Tzu*, VIII, 11

48. That is, your sword.

49. U (有), as opposed to *mu* (無), or Non-existence. Here it apparently means to watch the opponent's eyes.

> The entrance to victory, all actions, the mind and harmony are called Existence. In Existence, you do not stop while attacking, you do not stay in one place, and you do not relax. . . . This is one significance of Existence. In everything—attack, retreat, advance, evasion—this is the foundation of the martial arts. —*Himonshu*

50. Enliven the very depths of the mind: above, Abiding in repose; below, a mental state of Attack that cannot be seen. This is of prime importance. —*Himonshu*

51. The two levels are *shoju* (初重) and *goju* (後重). This is an allusion to the two levels of working through koans in Zen Buddhist training. Within the two levels of koans there are six further classifications.

52. Though you know all the various practices well, you will not be able to use them until you have expelled the four dispositions of drawing back, retreat, listlessness, and timidity. Treat these four as strong opponents, for it is said that there are no opponents stronger than these four. —*Himonshu*

53. *Shonen munen, shochaku muchaku* (渉念無念、渉着無着). Another Zen phrase. Munenori would have learned this vocabulary from his friend Takuan.

> The occurence of a single thought, or an attachment to something are both sicknesses. The mind of No-Mind arises when you expel attachment. This is the absolute ultimate. *Tsuki no sho*

54. *Nen ni wataru* (念に渉る). Literally, "crossing over," or "ferrying across a thought." —TRANS.

55. *Munen* (無念). No-Thought. —TRANS.

56. Lit., "He answered, saying . . . " Who this "he" might be is not indicated in the text, but the concepts in these sections are clearly those of Takuan.

57. The word *chaku* (着) presents several choices in translation. I have used both "attachment" and "fixation" for this concept as one or the other English word seemed to better represent the meaning. Buddhism generally considers *chaku* to be on three different levels: attachment to things, to ideas (including the idea of a 'self'), and to Nirvana. —TRANS.

58. This is an allusion to the nineteenth case of the *Wumenkwan* (in Japanese, *Mumonkan* 無門関), the thirteenth-century Chinese collection of Zen koans. This work—particularly this case—seems to have been well known to master swordsmen during Munenori's time, and its influence can also be seen in *The Book of Five Rings* by Munenori's great contemporary, Miyamoto Musashi. The case is important enough in the thought of Zen and swordsmanship to be quoted more fully:

> Nansen was asked by Joshu, "What is the Way?" Nansen said, "Your ordinary mind is the Way." Joshu said, "Can you track it down or not?" and Nansen replied, "As soon as you look for it, it departs." Joshu then asked, "If you can't look for it, how will you know that it's the Way?" Nansen said, "The Way is not bound to knowing or not knowing. Knowing is confusion; not knowing is being blindsided. If you truly arrive at the Way of no doubt, it is like a great void or vast vacuity. How can you force this into confirmation or negation?"

The phrase is also quoted in Chapter 28 of the *Ching-te ch'uan-teng Lu*— in Japanese, *Keitoku dentoroku* (景徳伝燈録)—records relating the deeds and words of over six hundred Zen masters, compiled in 1004:

> The Way does not use practice. Simply have no blots or stains. How can there be no blots or stains? It is just this: when you have the mind of life and death, when you have the plan of making something, it is all blots and stains. If you want to encounter the Way directly, the everyday mind is the Way. What we call the everyday mind makes nothing, does not distinguish plus or minus, does not grasp or throw away, finds nothing regular or irregular, and sees no secular or holy.   —TRANS.

59.   The Correct Mind manifests itself by extending the mind throughout the body. It is not biased in any one place. When the mind is biased in one place and lacking in another, it is called a one-sided mind. One-sidedness is despicable.   —*Fudochi shinmyoroku*

60. P'ang Yun, or P'ang Chu-shih (740–808). Dharma successor to Shiht'ou and Ma-tsu. Wandered China with his equally clever daughter, visiting famous Zen masters and engaging in "Zen conversations." His sayings are recorded in the *P'ang Chu-shih yu lu* (in Japanese, *Ho shikyo rongo*).   —TRANS.

61.   No-Mind is the same as Right Mind. It neither congeals nor fixes itself in one place. It is called No-Mind when the mind has neither dis-

crimination nor thought but wanders about the entire body and extends throughout the entire self.

No-Mind is located nowhere. It is not like wood or stone. Where there is no stopping place, it is called No-Mind. When it stops, there is something in the mind. When there is nothing in the mind, it is called the mind of No-Mind. It is also called No-Mind/No-Thought.

When this No-Mind has been well developed, the mind does not stop with one thing, nor does it lack any one thing. It is like water overflowing and exists within itself. It appears appropriately when facing a time of need. —*Fudochi shinmyoroku*

62. This according to the Zen sect.

63. Chung-feng (1263–1323). The Zen priest who converted the Yuan-period emperor Ying-tsung.

64. From Mencius, the great Confucian writer of the fourth century B.C.E.

This is a saying of Mencius. It means that one should seek out the lost mind and return it to himself. If a dog, cat, or cock has escaped and run off to some other place, one will look for it and return it to his house. Likewise, when the mind, the master of the body, has gone off on a wicked path, why do we not seek after it and restore it to ourselves? —*Fudochi shinmyoroku*

65. But there is also a saying of Shao K'ang-chieh's that goes, "It is essential to lose the mind." This is quite different. The general drift is that when the mind is tied down, it tires, and like a cat [on a string] is unable to function as it should. . . . Let it alone to run off wherever it will. —*Fudochi shinmyoroku*

66. In Confucianism, this word, *kei* (敬), has several different meanings, depending on the context and period in which it is discussed. Other basic meanings are "respect" and "seriousness."

The meaning of the word "reverence" is in holding the mind in check and not sending it off somewhere, thinking that if one did let it go, it would become confused. At this level there is a tightening up of the mind, and not one iota of negligence is allowed.

—*Fudochi shinkyoroku*

67. *Isshin furan* (一心不乱). One Mind without Confusion. —TRANS.

68. Fudo Myo-o (in Sanskrit, *Acalantha*), the Brightness King of Immovable

Wisdom. A manifestation of the central cosmic Buddha, Vairocana, and the central image of Takuan's *Fudochi shinmyoroku*, or *The Mysterious Record of Immovable Wisdom*. —TRANS.

69. Representing deeds, words, and thoughts.

70. This last section refers to esoteric Buddhism. In this practice, the body becomes the symbol or mudra, the mouth expresses the mystic sound or mantra, and the mind is absorbed in meditation.

71. In Buddhism, we also have the mentality of reverence. When a bell called the Bell of Reverence is rung three times, we place our hands together and do obeisance. This attitude of reverence, in which one first intones the name of the Buddha, is synonymous with having "one aim with no distractions" or "one mind without confusion."
—*Fudochi shinmyoroku*

72. Chung-feng also said, "Make no provision for retreat." This means to have a mind that will not be altered. —*Fudochi shinmyoroku*

73. Takuan.

THE LIFE-GIVING SWORD

1. [In the Shinkage-ryu], every time the sword is in stance, it is called the Death-Dealing Sword [or *satsuninto* 殺人刀]. When it is not in stance, it is called the Life-Giving Sword [*katsujinken* 活人剣]. Moreover, the sword in stance always cuts down the opposition and removes it; when it is not in stance, it gives life to the opposition and thus is called the Life-Giving Sword. —*Motsujimi shudan kudensho*

2. *Shuji shuriken* (手字種利剣). This term is somewhat vague, but as will be seen, it is a point on the opponent on which to fix your eyes and order to judge his actions and intent. *Shuji* may indicate the point on the opponent's upper chest where the lapels of his garment cross. As Munenori explains, *shuriken* (種利剣) is a sort of homonym for *shuriken* (手裏見), "looking behind the opponent's technique." Neither should be confused with *shuriken* (手裏剣), the dirk or bladed star used to throw at an opponent.

   This is a way of observing. If you fix your eyes on an unmoving point and mark it well, you will be able to see the movement of the *shuriken*.

By paying attention to the non-existent, you will be able to see the existent quite well. —*Tsuki no sho*

3. See the fifth chapter of Miyamoto Musashi's *The Book of Five Rings*.
—TRANS.

4. Commonly called the *Tao Te Ching*. Written in the fourth or fifth century B.C.E.

5. From the *Tao Te Ching*'s first chapter:

The tao that can be defined is not the Unchanging Tao,
The name that can be named is not the Unchanging Name.
The Nameless is the beginning of Heaven and Earth,
The named is the mother of the ten thousand things.
Thus, if you want Non-Existence in the Unchanging,
    look at its mysteries;
If you want Existence in the Unchanging,
    look at what's around you.

6. The opponent's height and my height: these are measured like the Lesson of Three Feet. —*Tsuki no sho*

The Moon on Water means the cast of your opponent's shadow. If you keep a distance from him equal to the cast of his height, he will not be able to strike you no matter how he attacks. —*Himonshu*

7. According to my father, this is called the *nakazumi* (中墨). It is the place where you hold the sword, an area of about five or six inches around the navel. The *shuri shujiken*, the Moon on Water, and the Mysterious Sword are all measured against the human body. They are the father and mother of the martial arts. —*Tsuki no sho*

8. Although written with different ideographs, sword (剣) and look (見), or observe, are both pronounced *ken* in Sino-Japanese. —TRANS.

9. *Shin* (神) and *myo* (妙) are the two ideographs making up the word "mysterious" in Mysterious Sword. In common usage, *shin* means "gods," "divine," or sometimes "mind" or "soul." *Myo* means "strange," "mysterious," "exquisite" or "charming." —TRANS.

10. Again, Munenori employs a sort of pun here to hint at layers of meaning. Both 神 (gods, divine) and 心 (heart/mind) are pronounced *shin*. Takuan notes,

This *shin* is in the body and is its master. It can be distinguished as "character" or "mind," but while each is a little different, in essence they are the same. There is *shin* within every person's body.

11. In the sense that it is conscious rather than unconscious.

12. When you hold your sword and want to strike, want to win, or want to fight—these three are a wasting of the mind and have their origins in sickness. All of these disconcert your actions with your own ego.

—*Himonshu*

13. Fixing your sight on the place where your eyes first stop. Defeating your opponent while not changing your gaze. —*Himonshu*

14. It is good to calm yourself before employing the Moon on Water. After stepping into that area, it is better to pick up the rhythm. The action of the feet should be light and quick, and the mind should not be cramped. —*Himonshu*

15. Facing the opponent directly; the Middle Posture.

16. All affairs and the ten thousand things are but One Principle. Because Principle exists in the One, there is the One Principle. —*Tsuki no sho*

17. My father said that you should not go beyond one foot in the extension or retraction of the sword, and that there should be no more than a foot between your fists that grasp the sword and aim with it, and the area of your Mysterious Sword. The tip of your sword should not extend more than one foot. Consider it essential when you strike to hold back and then strike maintaining this one-foot distance. —*Tsuki no sho*

18. These two ideographs always present the translator with interesting problems of shades of meaning. The ideograph for "insight," *kan* (観), actually means "to look," "to contemplate," or "to observe." Mahayana Buddhists, and especially the Zen sect, use this ideograph in combinations such as *kanshin* (観心), which means to meditate and see through to what the mind truly is. This is an "in-sight," non-conceptual and beyond words. The other ideograph, *ken* (見), translated here as "observation," depicts an eyeball with legs, indicating the active process of seeing or looking, and hence, observing. —TRANS.

19. *Kan* (観) is listening with the mind. It is seeing by closing the eyes and looking within. In *kan* there is no action. Actions will appear upon the

conditions set by the opponent. . . . There is no action or duplicity in *kan*; it is the very foundation of intent. It is the mind that sees most fundamentally. The mind must not stop at any one place. If it stops, it will not be stopping in *kan*. . . . *Ken* (見) is seeing in the present. Something is first seen with the eyes; it then passes along the consciousness and arrives at the mind. In seeing with the eyes, there is no action or creativity. It goes from the exterior to the interior. —*Musashino*

20. "Seeing through your own thoughts" in Japanese is *kannen* (観念).
—TRANS.

21.   During a match, there are places you strike and places you do not strike. This is the Moon on Water. You do not strike places other than the Moon on Water. Play with your opponent in various places outside of the Moon on Water, and you will see what he has in mind.
—*Shinkage-ryu heiho kokoromochi*

22.   This is the mental attitude of distinguishing place . . . It is essential to maintain this in the very depths of the mind.   —*Tsuki no sho*

23.   Although there are a variety of ways of brandishing the sword, these will be controlled from one place: this place is the Mysterious Sword.
—*Shinkage-ryu heiho kokoromochi*

24.   When the opponent takes the *gedan* or *chudan* stance, he will raise his sword overhead in a broad motion to strike. Let your sword follow in like manner and defeat him. It is good to have the mental attitude of following this action with your body.   —*Himonshu*

25. The Three Levels are the mind, the eyes, and the body and limbs.

26. Munenori specifically does not use Chinese characters here in order not to tie down the meaning of *utsuru*, which can mean either "move" (in which case it is written 移る) or "reflect" (written with the kanji 映る). Thus, the Japanese reader's mind can move freely between both meanings, or consider the meanings to be intended as layered.   —TRANS.

27.   To attack precipitously without first taking up the Moon on Water is no attack at all. You should receive your opponent, move to the Mysterious Sword, and strike from a stance of Abiding. . . . If you attack precipitously, you will be pushed too far and suffer loss with immediate regret.   —*Heiho sesso kokoromochi*

28. You must not stop your mind with strike after strike of your sword, but should return the mind and use it for complete mindfulness. This mental attitude is one of separating the mind and the strike.

—*Tsuki no sho*

29. There is such a thing as an interval into which not even a single hair can be put. We can speak of this in terms of your own martial art. "Interval" is when two things come one upon another, and not even a hair-breadth can be slipped in between them. When you clap your hands and, at the same instant, let out a yell, the interval between clapping your hands and letting out the yell will not allow the entrance of a hairsbreadth. This is not a matter of clapping your hands, thinking about yelling, and then doing so. You clap your hands and, at just that moment, let out a sound.

In the same way, if the mind stops with the sword with which a man is going to strike you, there will be an interval, and your own action will be lost. But if the interval between your opponent's striking sword and your own action is narrower than the breadth of a hair, your opponent's sword should become your own.

—*Fudochi shinmyoroku*

30. Arriving at the mental state of One Mind by expelling all thoughts of the techniques you have learned.

Thinking of your numerous practices is also a sickness, so you should expel them all and reach the mental state of One Mind. The One Expulsion is the realm of truth. —*Tsuki no sho*

31. The practice of seeing through the mental state of your opponent's first move. —TRANS.

32. *Boshin* (棒心). *Bo*, also pronounced *sasageru*, means to lift something up with both hands, as though making an offering or consecration.

My father said that in One Expulsion, the Rhythm of Emptiness is faster than fixing the eyes; and that the Firmly-held Mind is faster than Emptiness. —*Tsuki no sho*
—TRANS.

33. In Buddhism we abhor this stopping and the mind remaining with one thing or another. We call this stopping "affliction." It is like a ball

riding a swift-moving current: we respect the mind that flows on like this and does not stop for an instant in any place.

—*Fudochi shinmyoroku*

34. If the thought to strike arises, you will naturally grasp the hilt of your sword. As you do so, your elbow will tighten. Observe that tightness. Before you concentrate, if you do not make efforts to see the invisible place, you will not be able to see the opponent's mind.

—*Tsuki no sho*

35. "The place that may or may not move" is the mind that observes the place from which [the opponent's] mind emanates. It is essential to see this from the midst of Emptiness. It can be seen, even before it becomes visible, by using the mind.

—*Tsuki no sho*

36. *Koku* (虚空). Empty space.   —TRANS.

37. *Shinku* (真空). True Emptiness. Emptiness of actuality, the Void.   —TRANS.

38. *Shinku* (心空). Emptiness of the mind. This is yet another pun suggesting overlapping meanings. The phrase True Emptiness (真空) has the same pronunciation, *shinku*.   —TRANS.

39. Not having such a tactic, if one, in the end, becomes entangled and confused, he will damage his own blade or injure his own hand, and will fall short of adroitness. One does not divine this by impressions or knowledge. There is no transmitting it by words or speech, nor learning it by any doctrine. This is the law of the special transmission beyond instruction.

—*Taiaki*

40. The Right Mind is the mind that does not remain in any one place. It is the mind that strectches throughout the entire body and self.

—*Fudochi shinmyoroku*

41. Well then, the accomplished man uses the sword, but does not kill others. He uses the sword and gives others life. When it is necessary to kill, he kills. When it is necessary to give life, he gives life. When killing, he kills in complete concentration. When giving life, he gives life in complete concentration.   —*Taiaki*

42. This poem appears at the close of the *Fudochi shinmyoroku*.

43. Munenori's exegesis has been slightly abridged to allow for a smooth translation of the poem. The original poem runs:

> *Kokoro koso / kokoro mayowasu / kokoro nare / kokoro ni kokoro / kokoro yurusuna*
> (心こそ / 心まよはす / 心なれ / 心に心 / 心ゆるすな)
>
> —TRANS.

44. "What was your original face before your mother and father were born?" is a well-known Zen koan. Zen koan are paradoxical questions, or conundrums, posed by teachers to disciples to help them achieve enlightenment.

> Well then, the True Self is the self that existed before the division of Heaven and Earth, and before one's father and mother were born. This self is the self within me, the birds and the beasts, and the grasses and the trees and all phenomena. It is exactly what is called the Buddha-nature. —*Taiaki*
>
> —TRANS.

45. The so-called Fox Zen. Men who speak cleverly enough to convince others, and who have perhaps convinced even themselves.

46. When I was young, the activity of my blood was not yet settled.
    —*The Analects of Confucius*

47. The deluded mind thinks something over and congeals in one place. When the Original Mind congeals and settles into one place, it becomes what is called the deluded mind. When the Original Mind is lost, it is lacking in function here and there. Thus, it is important not to lose it. —*Fudochi shinmyoroku*

48. These two terms, Great Potential (*daiki* 大機) and Great Function (*daiyu* 大用) are commonly seen in Chinese philosophy and Buddhist thought, their meanings changing with the period, individual writer and particular school. Some writers prefer not to translate them at all, but rather let the reader infer their meanings from context. This translation attempts to come as close as possible to the meanings suggested by Munenori's text and other related works, but the reader should again keep a broad mind.

   In Zen there is a phrase, "Function follows Potential as swiftly as the wind," or *Daiki daiyu hayaki koto kaze no gotoshi* (大機大用疾如風). The *ki* of *daiki* refers to the inner workings of the mind, while the *yu* of *daiyu* refers to the actions that manifest those inner workings. —TRANS.

49. Substance here is 躰 or 体 (both are pronounced *tai*). This is the fundamental character of all things. —TRANS.

50.   The mentality of considering that the opponent's changes [literally, colors] issue forth from yourself is first in importance. The mind that follows the opponent's changes will actually be following at his heels. You will defeat him by first having the opponent follow your own changes, and then by following his. —*Himonshu*

51. "Great" in Japanese is *dai* (大). The Bright God, or *daimyojin* (大明神), Great Incarnation, or *daigongen* (大権現), and Great Bodhisattva, or *daibosatsu* (大菩薩) respectively. —TRANS.

52.   Therefore, this is called the doctrine of a "special transmission beyond instruction." This is a doctrine outside the teachings of an instructor, a doctrine that particularly requires self-enlightenment and realization on one's own. —*Taiaki*

53.   There is no established rule for manifesting Great Function. Orderly action, contrary action—even Heaven does not determine this. . . . If the Great Function of the law of this special transmission should manifest itself in front of you, it will do so freely, without the existence of any established rule. And yet it is called the Great Function because it extends in all the ten directions and is missing from no place, not even by the tip of a rabbit's hair. An established rule is a law or regulation, but there are no laws or regulations such as would mold things concerning the manifestation of this Great Function. —*Taiaki*

54. Munenori again using homonyms to overlap meanings. Both potential (機) and *ch'i* (気) are pronounced *ki* in Sino-Japanese. —TRANS.

55. That is, its location.

56. Manorhata: The twenty-second patriarch of Indian Zen Buddhism. An Indian prince who left his home at the age of thirty to become the disciple and successor of the great Buddhist philosopher, Vasubhandu. He lived in Western India and the central Asian kingdom of Ferghana, and died in 165 C.E. The second stanza of this verse, which he reportedly wrote for a nun, runs:

> Follow the current and recognize your nature;
> No rejoicing, no sorrow.

Sekishusai used this verse as a note to the concept of *shuji shuriken.*

57.	My mind shifts with everything it confronts. In the martial arts, we consider all our various workings—upper stance, lower stance, turning the Wheel, advancing in Attack, pulling back in Abiding—as the ten thousand circumstances. Shifting in accordance with the ten thousand circumstances entails not stopping the mind in one place. It entails watching the workings of the opponent, quickly shifting the mind that watches them, watching the opponent changing methods, and again not stopping the mind in the place it is watching, and knowing these changing actions.	*—Shinkage-ryu heisho*

58. The original poem is found in the *Shui waka shu*, the third Imperial anthology, compiled between 995 and 998 C.E. by Fujiwara no Kinto. The full poem, written by Shami Mansei (Kusa no Maro) during the eighth century, goes:

> To what shall I
>   compare this world?
> The white waves left
>   by the boat rowed away
>   in the faint-lit dawn.

There is an untranslatable pun here, as *shiranami*, or "white waves," could also be understood as "unknown," which fits Munenori's meaning well.
	—TRANS.

59.	It is not that man's mind has a form that cannot be seen by the eye. It is simply through his actions that his mind is manifested, and the mind that is within his breast is known on the outside. Nevertheless, the mind is manifested in the place to which it has shifted, and the traces of that shifting are undefined and difficult to see.—*Shinkage-ryu heisho*

60. Saigyo (1119–90). The wandering poet-priest had arrived at Eguchi, a district in Osaka, when he was caught without shelter during a rainstorm. He asked for lodging at a brothel, but was refused by a prostitute who, according to legend, was an incarnation of the Bodhisattva Fugen (Sanskrit, Samantabhadra), who is known as the personification of meditation and practice. Saigyo's poem ran:

> How difficult I suppose,
>   to reject
> This world of ours.

> And yet you begrudge me
> a temporary stay.
>
> —TRANS.

61. Lung-chi Shao-hsiu (1529–88). Ming-dynasty Buddhist priest.

62. Takuan.

63. It should be noted that *chu* (柱), or pillar, also means "main support" in Japanese as in English. In Buddhism it is thought that our concepts of Existence and Non-Existence are the main supports of our conception of reality, the "reality" to which we are so attached. Both are illusions in an absolute sense.   —TRANS.

64.   Without looking at right and wrong [Existence and Non-Existence], he is able to see right and wrong; without attempting to discriminate, he is able to discriminate well. . . . This means that concerning his martial art, he does not look at it to say, "correct" or "incorrect," but he is able to see which it is. He does not attempt to judge matters, but is able to do so quite well.   —*Taiaki*

65. All the lifelong disciplines that people follow. For example, *kyudo* (the Way of archery), *sado* (the way of tea), *karate-do* (the way of karate), *shodo* (the way of calligraphy), or *kendo* (the way of the sword).

> —TRANS.

66.   A certain man once said, "No matter where I put my mind, my intentions are held in check in the place where my mind goes, and I lose to my opponent. Because of that, I place my mind just below my navel and do not let it wander. Thus I am able to change according to the actions of my opponent."

   This is reasonable. But viewed from the highest standpoint of Buddhism, putting the mind just below the navel and not allowing it to wander is a low level of understanding, not a high one. It is at the level of discipline and training. It is at the level of "reverence."

> —*Fudochi shinmyoroku*

67. The first chapter ("The Shoe-Presenting Bridge") is concerned with the teachings of Kamiizumi Musashi no kami Hidetsuna. The latter two ("The Death-Dealing Sword" and "The Life-Giving Sword") are the further understanding of swordsmanship reached by Sekishusai and Munenori.

68. From Confucius's book on human nature:

> Obtaining a single good, he respectfully and carefully held it to his breast.
>
> *Ichizen o uru ni kenken fukuyosu*
> (得一善, 拳拳服膺)
>
> *—Doctrine of the Mean*

With this quote, Munenori compares himself to Hui (Yen Yuan), Confucius's favorite disciple, and his father to Confucius. Although Munenori's swordsmanship found its philosophical/psychological basis in Zen Buddhism, his relationship with his father and other elders was clearly informed by Confucianism. Takuan was also well versed in this ancient Chinese thought, and did not hestitate to lecture Munenori on its principles when he thought it necessary.

—TRANS.

69. At fifty, I knew Heaven's decree.
Goju ni shite tenmei o shiru
(五十而知天命)

—The Analects of Confucius

70. 1632 C.E.

71. If a man has tempered himself and arrived at these principles, he will control everything under Heaven. For those who study this, let them not take it lightly. *—Taiaki*

AFTERWORD

1. *Shugyosha* (修行者). Literally, "person in training." In this case, swordsmen who wandered the country doing ascetic practices, disciplining their bodies and honing their martial skills. There were a number of rules about the *shugyosha* lifestyle that were tacitly understood, but basically these men lived without money or many possessions, and engaged in martial contests whenever possible and proper. *—TRANS.*

ILLUSTRATED CATALOG OF THE SHINKAGE-RYU MARTIAL ARTS

1. These techniques have changed somewhat since Nobusada's time as the Yagyu Shinkage-ryu has split into a number of branches. Their titles have

for the most part remained the same, but each instructor will teach them according to his own school's understanding. Note that "An oral transmission" follows each paragraph, indicating that the instructions given in words are only the bare bones of the teaching.

2. The seventh generation of the heavenly gods. Through their marriage, they created the islands of Japan.

3. Goddess of the sun, born from the left eye of Izanagi. She is considered to be the first ancestor of the imperial family in Japan.

4. The sword is held over the right shoulder, pointing upward and to the rear.

5. Holding the sword in a high position with the hilt level with the right shoulder.

6. Parry (*tsumeru* 詰める): A stepping in and stifling of an attack or blow, or a deflection leading to a counter-strike. Not a simple block.

7. Each of the section titles indicate the name of a certain Tengu.